D0207492

Mozart: Piano Concertos
No. 20 in D minor, K. 466, and No. 21 in C major, K. 467

This guide to Mozart's two most popular piano concertos – the D minor, K. 466, and the C major, K. 467 (the so-called 'Elvira Madigan') – presents the historical background of the works and places them within the context of Mozart's compositional and performance activities at a time when his reputation as both composer and pianist was at its peak. The special nature of the concerto, as both a form and a genre, is explored through a survey of some of the approaches that critics have taken in discussing Mozart's concertos, ranging from analyses of pure structure to representations of the works as metaphors for human dramas. A theory of concerto form provides the basis for detailed accounts of the two concertos. The concluding chapter discusses a wide range of issues of particular interest to modern performers, including historical instruments, orchestra size and seating, cadenzas, basso continuo and improvised embellishments.

DAVID GRAYSON teaches musicology at the University of Minnesota. He is author of *The Genesis of Debussy's 'Pelléas et Melisande'*.

CAMBRIDGE MUSIC HANDBOOKS

GENERAL EDITOR Julian Rushton

Published titles

Bach: *The Brandenburg Concertos* MALCOLM BOYD
Bach: Mass in B Minor JOHN BUTT
Bartók: *Concerto for Orchestra* DAVID COOPER
Beethoven: *Missa solemnis* WILLIAM DRABKIN
Beethoven: *Eroica Symphony* THOMAS SIPE
Beethoven: *Pastoral Symphony* DAVID WYN JONES
Beethoven: Symphony No. 9 NICHOLAS COOK
Beethoven: Violin Concerto ROBIN STOWELL
Berg: Violin Concerto ANTHONY POPLE
Berlioz: *Roméo et Juliette* JULIAN RUSHTON
Brahms: Clarinet Quintet COLIN LAWSON
Brahms: *A German Requiem* MICHAEL MUSGRAVE
Brahms: Symphony No. 1 DAVID BRODBECK
Britten: *War Requiem* MERVYN COOKE
Chopin: The Four Ballades JIM SAMSON
Chopin: The Piano Concertos JOHN RINK
Debussy: *La mer* SIMON TREZISE
Gershwin: *Rhapsody in Blue* DAVID SCHIFF
Handel: *Messiah* DONALD BURROWS
Haydn: *The Creation* NICHOLAS TEMPERLEY
Haydn: String Quartets, Op. 50 W. DEAN SUTCLIFFE
Haydn: The 'Paris' Symphonies BERNARD HARRISON
Holst: *The Planets* RICHARD GREENE
Ives: *Concord Sonata* GEOFFREY BLOCK
Janáček: *Glagolitic Mass* PAUL WINGFIELD
Liszt: Sonata in B Minor KENNETH HAMILTON
Mahler: Symphony No. 3 PETER FRANKLIN
Mendelssohn: *The Hebrides* and other overtures R. LARRY TODD
Monteverdi: Vespers (1610) JOHN WHENHAM
Mozart: Clarinet Concerto COLIN LAWSON
Mozart: The 'Haydn' Quartets JOHN IRVING
Mozart: The 'Jupiter' Symphony ELAINE R. SISMAN
Musorgsky: *Pictures at an Exhibition* MICHAEL RUSS
Nielsen: Symphony No. 5 DAVID FANNING
Schubert: *Die schöne Müllerin* SUSAN YOUENS
Schumann: Fantasie, Op. 17 NICHOLAS MARSTON
Sibelius: Symphony No. 5 JAMES HEPOKOSKI
Strauss: *Also sprach Zarathustra* JOHN WILLIAMSON
Stravinsky: *Oedipus rex* STEPHEN WALSH
The Beatles: *Sgt Pepper's Lonely Hearts Club Band* ALLAN MOORE
Verdi: Requiem DAVID ROSEN
Vivaldi: *The Four Seasons* and other concertos, Op. 8 PAUL EVERETT

Mozart: Piano Concertos
No. 20 in D minor, K. 466, and
No. 21 in C major, K. 467

David Grayson

CAMBRIDGE
UNIVERSITY PRESS

PUBLISHED BY THE PRESS SYNDICATE OF THE UNIVERSITY OF CAMBRIDGE
The Pitt Building, Trumpington Street, Cambridge CB2 1RP, United Kingdom

CAMBRIDGE UNIVERSITY PRESS
The Edinburgh Building, Cambridge CB2 2RU, United Kingdom
40 West 20th Street, New York, NY 10011–4211, USA
10 Stamford Road, Oakleigh, Melbourne 3166, Australia

First published 1998

Printed in the United Kingdom at the University Press, Cambridge

Typeset in Ehrhardt MT 10½/13pt, in QuarkXPress™   [SE]

A catalogue record for this book is available from the British Library

Library of Congress cataloguing in publication data
Grayson, David A.
Mozart, Piano concertos no. 20 in D minor, K. 466, and no. 21 in C
major, K. 467 / David Grayson.
p.   cm. – (Cambridge music handbooks)
Includes bibliographical references and index.
ISBN 0 521 48156 2 (hardback) – 0 521 48475 8 (paperback)
1. Mozart, Wolfgang Amadeus, 1756–1791. Concertos, piano,
orchestra, K. 466, D minor.   2. Mozart, Wolfgang Amadeus,
1756–1791. Concertos, piano, orchestra, K. 467, C major.
I. Title.   II. Series.
ML410.M9G82   1998
784.2′62′092–dc21   97–50598   CIP MN

ISBN 0 521 48156 2 hardback
ISBN 0 521 48475 8 paperback

To my wife, Lydia
an incomparable Mozartian

Contents

Figures

Preface

Mozart was not my first musical love, but he has been the deepest and most enduring. I first came upon his piano concertos when barely in my teens in the course of acquainting myself with the "standard repertory" by systematically going through the record collection of the public library in Lexington, Massachusetts, where I grew up. At that time I responded most strongly to the recordings by Rudolf Serkin – his recordings of the 1950s and early 1960s with George Szell and Alexander Schneider. Inspired by his example, I tried to play some of the concertos myself, with decidedly mixed results. Almost a decade later, in the early 1970s, I was fortunate enough to meet Mr. Serkin at the Marlboro Music Festival in southern Vermont, where I worked for six summers, primarily as a recording engineer. I arranged my work schedule so I could turn pages for him at practically every rehearsal and performance. It was at Marlboro, and chiefly from spending so many hours sitting next to Mr. Serkin while he played with such intensity, passion, and concentration, that I learned what it meant to devote oneself to music. Although chamber music reigned at Marlboro, on rare occasions Mr. Serkin permitted himself a solo turn, in the process reminding us what a great virtuoso he was – although that was never his intent. Particularly memorable was a performance on 6 July 1975 of Mozart's Piano Concerto in B-flat, K. 595, with Alexander Schneider conducting the Festival Orchestra. Although he knew every note, at rehearsals Mr. Serkin regularly consulted a unique photocopy of the autograph, especially precious at the time since the actual manuscript had been lost during the Second World War. (The autograph has since been located and published in facsimile by Bärenreiter.) Aware of my keen interest in such things, he pointed out some details of Mozart's notation that were particularly meaningful to him and, following one rehearsal, handed me the score, asking if I would be willing to keep it for him until the next rehearsal. He knew, of course, that I was dying to look at it. (The sly poker face was a lesser-known facet of his sense of humor. On another occasion he played a rehearsal of a Haydn trio from a first edition and remarked afterward that the previous owner had apparently played only one of the trios in the volume, as it alone had fingerings marked in the score. "Do you know who owned it?" I asked innocently, ever the obliging straight man. "Maybe he wrote his name in the front," he replied, dramatically turning to the page bearing the signature of Felix Mendelssohn Bartholdy.)

After graduating from college I spent a year in Paris working with Nadia Boulanger, and in her analysis class we studied the Piano Concerto in C major, K. 467. My score of the work is filled with her wise observations. Then in graduate school I was fortunate to enroll in a seminar on the Mozart piano concertos taught by Christoph Wolff, who generously agreed to advise my dissertation. However, when I proposed topics in the areas of my greatest musical passions – Mozart and Beethoven – he pragmatically steered me toward Debussy, and I am glad to have followed his advice. While maintaining my scholarly interest in Debussy, I have found my way back to Mozart, just as Prof. Wolff predicted. In my current position on the faculty of the University of Minnesota I have offered seminars on the Mozart piano concertos, and I am grateful to the students in those classes, who shared their insights and stimulated my own thinking: Susan Becker, Andrew Chandler, Alejandro Cremaschi, Andrew Druckenbrod, Philip Ford, Joel Haney, William Intriligator, Timothy Jones, George Matthew, Mark Mazullo, Dale McGowan, Eric Mortensen, Katrina Mundinger, Tamara Norden, Daniel Rieppel, Sari Ronnholm, Helen Shively, and Aimee Tsuchiya. I must also thank my friend and colleague James Hepokoski, who, with Warren Darcy, is developing a theory of sonata form. Throughout this project Jim gave generously of his time and knowledge. When academic politics got us down – which has been often of late – we could always find refuge in Mozart. But whenever I came to an impasse in musical understanding or interpretation, the most reliable assistance came from my wife, the pianist Lydia Artymiw, an incomparable Mozartian and a musician with infallible instincts and the rare gift of being able to articulate them.

At Cambridge University Press I must thank, above all, Penny Souster for many kindnesses and much forbearance, and Professor Julian Rushton for his encouragement and sure guidance.

1

Introduction

"The D minor Concerto [of Mozart]," wrote Charles Rosen, "is almost as much myth as work of art: when listening to it, as to Beethoven's Fifth Symphony, it is difficult at times to say whether we are hearing the work or its reputation, our collective image of it."[1] Only when the performance is wanting, one is tempted to counter, but we know what he means. For Donald Francis Tovey the D-minor was "the most famous, the most perfect, and, if so disputable a term be worth risking, the greatest of all Mozart's concertos."[2] Some measure of its canonic status and its continual, if at times sporadic, prominence in the concert hall, reaching back to the early nineteenth century, may be taken from the number and stature of some of the composer–pianists who left their mark on the work (and vice versa) by composing cadenzas for it: Ludwig van Beethoven, John Baptist Cramer, Johann Nepomuk Hummel, Felix Mendelssohn,[3] Johannes Brahms, Clara Schumann, Anton Rubinstein, Charles Alkan, Carl Reinecke, Ferruccio Busoni, and Alfredo Casella. Brahms, though cynical about the capacity of the general audience "to understand or respect the best things," nevertheless remarked in 1878 that "the public always listen to [Mozart's] D minor [Concerto] . . . with reverence."[4]

Today, the C-major Piano Concerto, K. 467, is no less popular, owing in no small part to the effective use of bits of its slow movement in the 1967 Swedish film *Elvira Madigan*. For better or worse, the "Elvira Madigan" nickname seems to have stuck. It remains a useful "hook" for concert and CD promoters, and audiences seem to respond to it still, even though the film itself is by now a distant memory. The C-major Concerto has also attracted a new generation of cadenza writers, notably, in the 1980s, Alfred Schnittke and Philip Glass. It makes a logical pairing with the D-minor Concerto, as the two were composed consecutively, between mid January and early March 1785. This simultaneous, or near simultaneous, gestation of contrasting minor and major works in the same genre has its counterparts in other notable masterpiece pairs, most prominently the C-major and G-minor String Quintets, K. 515 and 516, of April and May 1787, and the G-minor and C-major ("Jupiter") Symphonies, K. 550 and 551, of July and August 1788.[5] Dark and light, tragic and comic, call it what you will. It is as if a compositional impulse of operatic proportions, too large and too rich to be contained within a single instrumental work, required a complementary pair for its adequate expression. Or perhaps there was some deeper psychological motivation, a simultaneous need to express and purge one of the bouts of melancholia to which he was prone.[6] As he explained in a letter of June 1788, a month before composing the G-minor and "Jupiter" Symphonies, he suffered from "black thoughts," which he was able to banish only "by a tremendous effort."[7]

Mozart wrote only two concertos in minor keys, the only other one being the Piano Concerto in C minor, K. 491, of March 1786. His choice of D minor as the particular minor key for K. 466 may have had a quite specific significance. Martin Chusid surveyed the D-minor vocal numbers in Mozart's dramatic works and found that all five represented "a single dramatic situation: vengeance, either administered by the gods or sworn with the gods as witnesses."[8] Stuart Feder argued further that Mozart's D-minor works, both vocal and instrumental, may be biographically linked as reflections of his relationship with his father and, by extension, of his attitude toward fathering and fatherhood. Feder thus interpreted the D-minor "affects of rage and vengeance" as the "displacement" of Mozart's anger toward his "controlling father." In that regard he noted that K. 466 was written in anticipation of Leopold's visit to Vienna and, indeed, had its first performance the very day he arrived.[9] When we think of Mozart's most striking and expressive uses of D minor in his mature dramatic works, other commonalities emerge. Electra's aria in Act I of *Idomeneo* ("Tutte nel cor vi sento": "Furies of Hades, I feel all of you in my heart . . ."); the Act II aria of the Queen of the Night in *Die Zauberflöte* ("Der Hölle Rache": "The wrath of hell seethes in my heart"); in Act I of *Don Giovanni*, during Giovanni's mortal combat with the Commendatore ("Misero! attendi se vuoi morir!": "Poor wretch, stay then, if you wish to die!"), and in the Act II

Finale, when Giovanni refuses to repent and, taunted by a demonic chorus and consumed by flames, faces the terrors of hell; and add to these the opening movements of the Requiem – Introit ("Requiem aeternam": "Grant them eternal rest, O Lord"), Kyrie, and Dies irae ("Day of wrath, that day will dissolve the earth in ashes"): all are associated not merely with vengeance, but with death, hell, and (in secular contexts) the demonic.

For obvious reasons, connecting these quite specific affects and images to Mozart's "abstract" instrumental compositions in D minor is both more speculative and dangerously reductive, particularly when we are dealing with large-scale, topically varied, multi-movement works, like the String Quartets, K. 173 and K. 421, or even multisectional ones, like the Fantasia for Piano, K. 397/385g, and the three-part "Symphony," K. 118/74c, which served as the overture to *La Betulia liberata* (though the oratorio's plot line, highlighted by Judith's beheading of Holofernes, is certainly suggestive).

C major has its own history of associations,[10] but in the context of Mozart's minor–major pairs its essential virtue seems to be its apparent neutrality. With neither sharps nor flats in its key signature, it symbolizes the absence of preconditions and consequently suggests an unlimited and unfettered creative potential. It presents a *tabula rasa* inviting and conducive to displays of compositional virtuosity, which almost invariably means counterpoint, as Mozart demonstrated so masterfully in his "ultimate" symphony, the "Jupiter."[11] K. 467 shares this same quality, though to a lesser degree.

Mozart wrote the Piano Concertos, K. 466 and 467, for his own use during the 1785 Lenten season, a period of hectic concert activity. He began K. 466 during the third week of January, immediately after he had completed the String Quartets in A major, K. 464, and C major (the so-called "Dissonant" or "Dissonance" Quartet), K. 465, the last of the six quartets later dedicated to Franz Joseph Haydn. The D-minor Concerto, K. 466, was completed on 10 February, the day before its première, which was given at the first in a series of six weekly concerts that Mozart was presenting at the Mehlgrube on successive Friday nights. These concerts proved to be quite lucrative, attracting more than 150 subscribers, each of whom paid a *souverain d'or* for the series. (As a point of reference, Mozart's annual rent for his "upper-bracket" furnished apartment was 460 gulden, or around 35 *souverains d'or*. Of course he had expenses connected with the concert series, including payments to the orchestra musicians, though the hall rental for each concert was only half a *souverain d'or*.[12]) When Leopold Mozart arrived at 1 p.m. on the day of the concert, to begin a visit that was to last more than ten weeks, the copyist was still preparing the concerto parts, so the orchestra had no opportunity to rehearse the finale. Still, according to Leopold, "the concert was magnificent and the orchestra played splendidly."[13] The following day, 12 February, Haydn paid a visit and was entertained with performances of three of the string quartets that Mozart later dedicated to him. It was on this occasion that Haydn told Leopold, "Before God and as an honest man I tell you that your son is the greatest composer known to me either in person or by name. He has taste and, what is more, the most profound knowledge of composition." In addition to presenting his own subscription series, Mozart performed his piano concertos at concerts organized by others in the Burgtheater: K. 456, presumably, on the 13th (lauded by the Emperor Joseph II with a shout of "Bravo, Mozart!"), and an "encore" performance of K. 466 on the 15th ("Magnifique," according to Leopold). Other concerts followed, both public and private, though Mozart may not have been remunerated for all of these "guest" appearances. Leopold inferred as much when he commented, in the context of his financial reckonings, "as a favour he has been playing frequently at other concerts in the theatre." To supplement his Mehlgrube series and capitalize on his ever-growing reputation, Mozart rented the Burgtheater on 10 March for a program of his own, the occasion for the première of K. 467. Its autograph manuscript is dated "February 1785," but Mozart entered the concerto in his personal thematic catalogue under 9 March, the day before the première. Judging from his report, Leopold's interest in this event was largely mercenary – that it brought in 559 gulden, more than expected. But to be fair to Leopold, he seems, after a month in Vienna, to have been exhausted by Wolfgang's busy schedule. "We never get to bed before one o'clock," he complained. "Every day there are concerts; and the whole time is given up to teaching, music, composing and so forth . . . If only the concerts were over! It is impossible for me to describe the rush and bustle."

Viewed in the context of Mozart's five primary sources of income – patronage, commissions (especially of operas), publications, concertizing, and teaching – the piano concerto performances emerge as the vehicle that put his primary musical talents, as composer and pianist, before the largest public in the most immediate and dramatic way. This is fitting, in that the temptation to regard the concerto as a metaphor for the interaction of an individual and some social group is practically irresistible. Tovey put it this way in his classic essay "The Classical Concerto":

> Nothing in human life and history is much more thrilling or of more ancient and universal experience than the antithesis of the individual and the crowd; an antithesis which is familiar in every degree, from flat opposition to harmonious reconciliation, and with every contrast and blending of emotion, and which has been of no less universal prominence in works of art than in life. Now the concerto forms express this antithesis with all possible force and delicacy.[14]

The eighteenth-century theorist Heinrich Christoph Koch made just such an analogy, though he drew his metaphor not from "real life" but from another art form, when he portrayed the concerto soloist as an actor in ancient Greek drama and the orchestra as the chorus: "[The soloist] expresses his feelings to the orchestra, and it signals him through short interspersed phrases sometimes approval, sometimes acceptance of his expression, as it were. Now in the allegro it tries to stimulate his noble feelings still more; now it commiserates, now it comforts him in the adagio."[15]

Other social models have also been advanced. Susan McClary, for example, sought to historicize the Classical concerto when she described it as the enactment "as a spectacle [of] the dramatic tensions between individual and society, surely one of the major problematics of the emerging middle class." Having thus paid lip service to historical contextualization, she went on to propose a concerto narrative that was a thoroughly modern and politically charged tale of an alienated, even marginalized, individual forced to submit to the will of a repressive social order.[16] Helen Shively offered an intriguing corrective to such reductionist adversarial scenarios by providing precisely the historical grounding neglected by McClary. She found it in Jürgen Habermas's notion of the eighteenth-century "public sphere," those emerging bourgeois outlets and institutions – like journals, salons, coffeehouses, and Masonic lodges – that permitted the public expression of individual, private, subjective thought through reasoned discourse, which thus had the capacity to shape politics and culture. By analogy, Shively viewed the relationship between the concerto soloist and the orchestra as one of mutual influence, with the former able to enter the "public sphere" without loss of autonomy and capable of transforming the social order.[17] Mozart himself joined such a "public sphere" on 14 December 1784, when he was admitted to the Masonic lodge "Zur Wohlthätigkeit" ("Charity"). K. 466 and K. 467 were thus the first piano concertos he wrote as a Freemason, and shortly after the première of the latter, on 26 March, he completed a setting of the Masonic song "Lied zur Gesellenreise," K. 468, intended for the installation of new journeymen. On 11 February 1785, the day K. 466 had its première, Mozart formally applied for membership in another important Viennese organization, the Tonkünstler-Societät (Musicians' Society), founded in 1771 to provide pensions for the families of its deceased members. At the Society's request, Mozart offered his cantata *Davidde penitente*, K. 469, for performance at their fundraising concerts on 13 and 15 March. Though largely adapted from music written for his unfinished Mass in C minor, K. 427/417a, the cantata contains two new arias, "A te, fra tanti affanni" (No. 6) for tenor, completed on 6 March, and "Fra l'oscure ombre funeste" (No. 8) for soprano, completed on March 11, the day after the première of K. 467. Action on Mozart's application to the Society was permanently suspended owing to his failure to submit his baptismal certificate. As a result, following his death in 1791, his widow was denied the pension to which she would otherwise have been entitled.

Joseph Kerman advanced a social model connected with Mozart's professional life when he suggested that "the solo part and the orchestral part in a concerto and their relationship can be read as a composite metaphor for Mozart and his audience and *their* relationship." Despite a certain appeal, this model seems both too literal and too restrictive to explain a repertory so rich and varied. In Kerman's reading, Mozart's concertos project "a single pervading myth" of comedy, tracing in their three movements a progression "from *interaction* to some sort of *respite* to *complicity*": "the individual is incorporated into society and society is transformed."[18] This formulation may be generally valid, but it is also overly general. And even if divorced from the more commercial aspects of the Mozart/Audience metaphor, it tends to reduce the concerto to a ritualistic reenactment of a single theme, no matter how culturally significant. But the concerto is more an opera, varied in plot and rich in incident, than a Mass or Masonic initiation ceremony, and while we may enjoy imagining Mozart as a universal celebrant or initiate, we would not want him portraying every operatic protagonist. Cherubino is no Don Giovanni, nor is Despina a Queen of the Night. Kerman is right to overturn the adversarial scenario with which the concerto is too often identified, and his insightful analyses are sensitive to the sundry and nuanced twists in the relationship between solo and orchestra. But to pursue the operatic analogy, the latter is not a monolithic force, but a variegated one out of which individual voices and factions may emerge. When Mozart opened the Piano Concerto in B-flat, K. 450, with obbligato winds it was not merely to announce his expanded orchestral palette, but to introduce a new group of "characters" who would make for ever more intricate concerto "plots."[19] Social models are very appealing because they translate the music into concrete, human terms, but we must remember that these metaphors are merely a way of understanding the music; they are not what the music *is*, nor even what it is *about*.

Other ways of explaining or contextualizing the concertos, speculative in different ways, have also been pursued. Some scholars have sought the historical origins of Mozart's concerto style in that of his predecessors and contemporaries, though for reasons largely unrelated to documented influence, attention has focused on north Germany and the most prominent members of the Bach family, Johann Sebastian and his "pre-Classical" sons, Carl Philipp Emanuel and Johann Christian.[20] Other scholars have turned to descriptions of concerto form by eighteenth-century theorists, above all H. C. Koch, to suggest how Mozart might have conceived the form and how his audience, in turn, might have perceived it.[21] Still others, mindful of an obvious parallel between instrumental and vocal soloists, have pursued connections between concerto and opera.[22] The essential paradox is that in form Mozart's concerto movements resemble the older *opera seria* aria, but in style they are more like the newer *opera buffa*. Such a mixture of the old and new characterizes other aspects of the Mozart piano concertos as well and, depending upon one's perspective, either contributes to their complexity and appeal or constitutes a "problem." Basso continuo and improvised embellishment, performance practices that we associate with the

Baroque, remain pertinent to Mozart's piano concertos even though they might seem anachronistic in the context of Classical instrumental music. Structurally, too, Mozart's concerto movements involve an interplay and special synthesis of two apparently contradictory formal models: ritornello form (drawn from the Baroque concerto model) and sonata form (or style, the characteristic constructive principle of the Classical era).

These two issues – form and performance practice – are the primary focuses of the present study of K. 466 and K. 467. Performance practices might seem peripheral to the study of a musical "work," but in the case of the Mozart piano concertos they bear directly on the nature of the interaction of solo and orchestra, which is at the very heart of the concerto genre. Performance-related issues have recently come to the fore through the activism of the "early music" movement, with its advocacy for "authentic" or "historically informed" performance. This has been made manifest to mass audiences chiefly, though not exclusively, through "period-instrument" recordings. Ralph Kirkpatrick, a pioneer in this regard, used a fortepiano (by John Challis) for his 1951 Haydn Society recording of the Piano Concerto in G, K. 453, and his example has since been followed on commercial recordings by other fortepianists, prominent among them Jörg Demus, Malcolm Bilson, Steven Lubin, Melvyn Tan, John Gibbons, Jos van Immerseel, Robert Levin, and Andreas Staier. These recordings with fortepiano are almost invariably with "period-instrument" orchestras, a characterization which can, of course, mean many different things. Even beyond the instruments themselves (and the associated "historically informed" playing techniques), important questions arise concerning orchestra size, seating, and ripieno practice (i.e., using the "full" orchestra for tuttis and a "reduced" orchestra to accompany solo sections). Additional historically sanctioned practices pertain to the solo. The options to embellish melodies (especially in slow movements), to provide basso continuo during tuttis, and to improvise cadenzas and lead-ins not only affect what notes we actually hear, but alter the nature of the solo–tutti contrast and thus influence the way in which soloist and orchestra are perceived as interacting. These and other performance-related topics will be discussed in detail in the final chapter.

Analytical discussions of Classical concerto form, from the mid eighteenth century to the present, have focused on several related issues. One key question has concerned the function of the opening orchestral tutti, reflected in the terminology used to describe it. Is it, by analogy with the Baroque concerto, a ritornello preceding the first solo? Or, by analogy with Classical sonata form, is it an introduction preceding a sonata-form movement, or the first of two expositions, the second of which will be presented by the solo (the "double exposition" model)?[23] Similar questions extend to the subsequent tuttis. Do they too function as ritornellos, or are they simply sections of textural contrast within an overall sonata structure? Divorcing the issues from an historical perspective, these competing views can be translated into more neutral terminology: Is concerto form defined primarily by texture, or by harmonic and thematic organization? Jane R. Stevens has pursued these very issues in a valuable survey of descriptions of concerto first-movement form which she culled from theoretical writings ranging from the mid eighteenth century through the mid twentieth.[24]

These three elements – texture, theme, and harmony – constitute the "core" parameters in any discussion or diagrammatic representation of Classical concerto structure. While Mozart's concertos show a general consistency in their harmonic organization (sonata-based) and textural distribution (derived from ritornello form yet responsive to sonata structure), the arrangement and rearrangement of thematic units defy easy schematization. Indeed, Mozart's concertos may well represent the pinnacle of his ingenuity in this regard. We might consider it in relation to *ars combinatoria*, a mathematical term which, when applied to music, refers to the interchangeability of melodic elements at different structural levels.[25] This principle was invoked in a number of eighteenth-century composition treatises in demonstrations of how to construct melodies out of different permutations of pitch patterns, figures, or phrases. It also found expression in certain musical games, in which simple dance pieces were created through the random arrangement of interchangeable "pre-fabricated" phrases, their choice and order determined by tossing dice. Mozart himself devised such a game in 1787, the *Musikalische Würfelspiel* ("Musical Dice-Game"), K. Anh. 294d/516f,[26] and the finale of his "Jupiter" Symphony carries the principle to an unprecedented level of brilliance, with the permutations of thematic units laid out in both horizontal and vertical dimensions. (Contrapuntal permutations are also prominent in the development section of the first movement of the other C-major masterpiece mentioned above, the String Quintet, K. 515.) In Johann Stamitz's symphonies of the 1750s, the virtually interchangeable thematic modules of the expositions are often rearranged in the recapitulations, to slightly surprising and mildly pleasurable effect. In contrast, when Haydn, later in the century, reorganizes his recapitulations, the results are breathtaking, or witty, because of striking new juxtapositions and continuities, and because the apparent functions of familiar materials have undergone transformation – hence the famous "joke" at the end of his "Joke" Quartet, Op. 33 No. 2, when the opening phrase makes for a witty ending. In comparison with Haydn, Mozart's symphony recapitulations tend to be far more regular, but the same can hardly be said of the piano concertos as a group. Accounting for the seeming unpredictability in thematic return, and not merely in the "recapitulation," is an important analytical issue that relates both to the overall design and to the dramatic interaction of solo and orchestra.

The literature on Mozart's piano concertos is vast, and analytical studies abound. However, for the present study of K. 466 and K. 467, with its focus on the formal issues outlined above, three positions representing a particular line of Anglo-American thinking seem central and unavoidable: those of Donald Francis Tovey, of Charles Rosen, and of Daniel Leeson and Robert Levin jointly.[27] These three general theories of Classical concerto form will be summarized and critiqued in Chapter 2, and then applied in the succeeding chapters to the two concertos in question.

2

Twentieth-Century theories of Mozart's concerto form

Donald Francis Tovey

Donald Francis Tovey's influential 1903 essay "The Classical Concerto" was reprinted in 1936 as the introductory article in the "Concertos" volume (vol. 3) of his *Essays in Musical Analysis*, where it preceded individual analyses of fifty concertos, ranging chronologically from the Classical era (Mozart and Haydn) to the early 1930s (Sir Arthur Somervell).[1] Ostensibly an introduction to the classical concerto, the essay also had other objectives stemming from its original function as a program note for a concert given in London on 4 November 1903 by the Queen's Hall Orchestra, conducted by Henry Wood. On that occasion Tovey was soloist, not only in Mozart's Piano Concerto in C Major, K. 503, the apparent focus of the essay, but also in his own Piano Concerto in A Major, Op. 15, which had its première on that occasion. In the essay Tovey claimed prestige for the classical concerto as "a highly dramatic and poetic art-form," which he felt was misunderstood, owing to the widespread and misleading "popular and pseudo-academic idea of the form," and undervalued, owing to "current criteria" for the genre, which mistakenly held "that the professed purpose of the form is technical display." He praised Mozart as responsible for "a good two-thirds" of the "hardly thirty perfect examples" of "true concerto form" known to him, and he lamented that Mozart's music had long "been treated with neglect and lack of intelligent observation, for which we at the present time are paying dearly with a notable loss both of ear for fine detail and of grasp of musical works as definite wholes." The essay is thus as much a defense of Mozart as a justification of Tovey's own compositional effort, for he considered the "classical" concerto a category that transcended the eighteenth century and represented a continuous, living tradition encompassing both Mozart's concertos and his own, while excluding many others. He thus divided the analyses in his *Essays* volume into two sections: "Concertos in Classical Form" (including not only Mozart, Haydn, and Beethoven, but Chopin, Joachim, Brahms, Dvořák, Elgar (for violin), and Somervell) as opposed to "Variations and Concertos Without Ritornello" (including, among others, Mendelssohn, Schumann, Saint-Saëns, Delius, Elgar (for cello), Sibelius, and Walton). This classification system identified unambiguously what Tovey considered to be the defining feature of the classical concerto: the ritornello.

It was one of the tenets of Tovey's analytical belief system that musical form was not a pre-existent "jelly-mould" into which musical materials are poured, but rather the "organic" result of the interaction of musical contents and principles. In keeping with this perspective, the first section of his essay offers a definition of the "concerto principle," followed by an historical survey, highly selective, of works which exemplify it, i.e., those whose "form is adapted to make the best effect expressible by opposed and unequal masses of instruments or voices." This survey leads to Mozart through a series of Baroque examples: Handel and Alessandro Scarlatti arias and Bach concertos and choruses. Through them Tovey refines and explores this definition, while laying out some of the significant "recurring features" of concerto style, which in his view are the logical and expressive consequence of the concerto principle. Despite the quasi-historical organization of the argument, Tovey is less interested in uncovering historical developments or trends than in elucidating the aesthetic, expressive, and psychological basis for the genre's nature and conventions. Being "the right thing in the right place," these conventions are universal, neither grounded in nor limited by history.

Basic to Tovey's discussion is the function of the opening ritornello. He argues that it is an effective way to create an impression of equality between forces of unequal dynamic capacity: it allows the orchestra to establish its presence and power, so that when it recedes into the background for the solo entry, the soloist is able to achieve and sustain a comparable prominence without the orchestra seeming to be "unnaturally repressed." Ritornellos subsequent to the first serve a different function, in Tovey's view. The solo "is probably more active, as well as more personal and eloquent, than the orchestra," but while the solo part can "make a brilliant climax," it lacks the latter's volume. Therefore, when the solo "climaxes" in a key (to signify a harmonic arrival), the orchestra "introduces parts of its [opening] ritornello" in that key to supply the element of sonic force that the solo lacks. In addition to these main texturally defined divisions, the orchestra may respond immediately to the initial solo utterance, thus creating "a more subtle relation" between them by having the solo first "enter into dialogue with the orchestra – the speaker should conciliate the crowd before breaking into monologue." Tovey found the source of this strategy in the motto opening common in Scarlatti's arias, though the principle is generalized and universalized by analogy with the tactics of public speaking. In Bach's concertos, Tovey observed, the solo often enters with new material, thus giving "new meaning" to the ritornello theme when "the orchestra breaks in on the first solo with Scarlatti's interruption (or something to that effect)."

Having identified the concerto principle through Baroque examples, Tovey then takes up the "Sonata-Form Concerto." One of his primary interests is to understand and justify the retention of the opening ritornello, that portion of the Classical concerto which would seem to be extraneous to sonata design (and which was often dispensed with in the "post-Classical" concerto). Again, Tovey maintains the universality of the concerto principle, arguing that, in comparison with the Baroque concerto, important features of sonata style – the greater range of movements, the obligatory opposition of materials, and the necessarily more dramatic treatment of both the larger and instrumentally more varied orchestra and the correspondingly more brilliant solo – not only make the opening ritornello more essential in the Classical concerto, but require that it be even longer.

Other concerto universals are suggested in the course of an extended analysis of a particular example, Mozart's Piano Concerto in C Major, K. 503, which had shared the 1903 program with Tovey's own Piano Concerto. Characteristically, Tovey's analysis makes few formal presumptions, but rather explores the formal consequences of applying the concerto principle to sonata form. His motto is: "All that we can be sure of is that nothing will be without its function, and that everything will be unexpected and inevitable." Above all, he seeks to overturn the "standard treatise" description of the Classical concerto, which, though unnamed, seems to be Ebenezer Prout's theory of the "double exposition," introduced in his *Applied Forms* of 1895 and thereafter widely adopted.[2] Tovey takes pains to underscore the differences between a symphonic exposition and a concerto ritornello. Far from being a "first exposition," the ritornello has "much the effect of an *introduction*": it cannot lead "to something with a beginning of its own, but . . . must be a preparation for some advent." The ritornello's "fixity of key" (i.e., the tonic key) "stamps the introductory ritornello character of the music more and more firmly the longer it continues." It also differs from a "first exposition" in often omitting the theme which is to become the second subject of the first solo. Few other "conventions" are detailed. Some, such as the effect of beginning the first solo with a "new theme" (relevant to K. 466 and K. 467 as well as K. 503) or the functions of the ritornellos subsequent to the first, are explicated in terms of the universal concerto principle, as already observed in the Baroque antecedents. Specific to the sonata-form Classical concerto, however, is Tovey's observation that the recapitulation is of both the opening ritornello and the first solo. "In particular, it is likely to follow the course of the opening [ritornello] much more closely than in the first solo" and to include "in the recapitulation of the second subject a theme from the ritornello that was not represented in the original solo statement."

The second and third movements of the Mozart concerto are treated more summarily, but not without great insights. Again, Tovey appeals to the concerto principle to explain how they differ from first-movement form, arguing that the solo has a different relationship with the orchestra: having already "won its way into friendship with the orchestral crowd" in the first movement, it can no longer achieve so great an effect through its entrances. Thus, "the relation of solo and tutti [is made] more intimate and less contrasted in middle and final than in first movements." Further, the forms tend to be more sectional, inviting a simpler type of alternation between solo and orchestra.

Charles Rosen

It is, of course, too facile to attribute Tovey's view of music as self-generating solely to his post-Brahmsian compositional project. As Mark Evan Bonds rightly points out, Tovey stands in a long tradition of theorists espousing an "organic-generative concept of form,"[3] and the tradition continues to the present, notably to Charles Rosen, whose post-Toveyan analyses may be associated with his sympathy, as a performer, for serial music, a style essentially defined by organic-generative principles.[4]

Charles Rosen took up the Classical concerto in both *The Classical Style: Haydn, Mozart, Beethoven* (1971, rev. 1972, 1997) and *Sonata Forms* (1980, rev. 1988). An entire chapter of the earlier book is devoted to Mozart's concertos. Rosen proceeds not by regarding the Classical concerto as a "fusion of the new sonata form and the older concerto form," but by exploring "how the functions of a concerto (the contrast of two kinds of sound, the display of virtuosity) are adapted to the new [sonata] style." Also like Tovey, he identifies a "concerto principle" based on the psychology of perception, though Rosen's formulation is even more "reader-oriented": "The most important fact about concerto form is that the audience waits for the soloist to enter, and when he stops playing they wait for him to begin again." The opening ritornello, in Rosen's view, therefore "conveys an introductory atmosphere" but is not a true introduction, since its harmonic character is that of a tonic rather than dominant chord. Although he embraces the "double-exposition" terminology he emphasizes the differences between concerto practice and the exposition repeat of sonata form: the ritornello is harmonically "passive," remaining throughout in the tonic, while the first solo is "active," the "dramatic modulation" being entrusted to the soloist. Moreover, "the solo exposition is an expansion and a transformation" of the orchestral exposition. The transformational process is one of dramatization and includes both "development (thematic fragmentation and extension) and modulation (large-scale harmonic opposition or dissonance)." The first solo characteristically closes with brilliant passage-work based on conventional patterns, the virtuosity conveying the essence of the concerto style and the conventional patterning contributing to the stability of the concluding cadence.

The first solo is followed by a tutti. While Tovey explained it through his concerto principle (i.e., the orchestra accorded the harmonic arrival the dynamic force that the solo lacked), Rosen stresses the thematic element and the sonata-style function – that the orchestra, by repeating the closing phrases of the opening ritornello, secures a needed symmetry between the two expositions. Rosen thus calls this section the "cadential tutti" and conceives it as part of the solo exposition. In fact, Rosen's thematic diagram of the first movement of Mozart's Piano Concerto in E-flat, K. 271, identifies its sections by the traditional sonata-form labels: orchestral exposition, solo exposition, development, recapitulation, and coda (including the cadenza). Again like Tovey, Rosen brings few formal preconceptions to his analyses, believing as he does that Mozart did the same in composing: "[He] bound himself only by the rules he reset and reformulated anew for each work."

When Rosen revisited the Classical concerto in Chapter 5 of *Sonata Forms*, he took a different tack. Rather than impose a sonata-form model on the concerto, as he had done in *The Classical Style*, he now diagrams concerto movements in terms of textural contrast, the alternation of solo and orchestra, arguing that around the middle of the eighteenth century concerto first-movement form became "rationalized" according to a design exemplified by Johann Christian Bach, consisting of "three solos framed by four tutti or ritornelli" and adhering to a stereotypical harmonic plan:[5]

R1	S1	R2	S2	R3	S3	R4
I	I→V	V	→vi	I	I	I

Nonetheless, Rosen continues to de-emphasize historical trends and evidence in favor of a speculative reconstruction of the "rational" composer's imperative solutions to compositional "problems," conundrums, and exigencies. He addresses three main formal issues – the relationship between the first tutti and first solo, the nature of the first solo, and the framing functions of the ritornellos. For the opening tutti he posits two principal harmonic alternatives – remaining throughout in the tonic (as in a Baroque concerto) or modulating to the dominant (as in a sonata exposition) – and identifies the former as preferable, given the "need" for overall symmetry (i.e., for the outer ritornellos to end identically). The greater length of the first ritornello (in comparison with Baroque antecedents) made it impractical for this section to be repeated in its entirety at the end of the movement, but the desired symmetry could still be achieved by having these outer tuttis end with the same themes and in the same key, necessarily the tonic since the movement obviously had to end in that key. It was therefore desirable for the opening ritornello not only to begin but to end in the tonic key. Its clear tonic close also helped to set it off from the first solo. There was admittedly a risk of tonal monotony if the tonic was maintained throughout the ritornello, but this could be averted by a modulation in the middle, hence the common pattern of modulating to the dominant for a second group of themes and then returning to the tonic for the closing. While solving one problem this scheme creates another. The chief drawback is that it introduces an element of harmonic tension and then resolves it, all within the opening ritornello, thus giving the impression of an "action completed," whereas having the ritornello refrain from modulating "implies that something will happen" and thus creates anticipation for the solo entrance. Moreover, it reserves the modulation to the dominant, which is the initial dramatic action, for the first solo. Though Mozart did use the modulating ritornello in rare instances (notably, the Piano Concerto in E-flat, K. 449), his preference was for the older, non-modulating design, which he "enlivened" in a number of ways, including the use of a theme that moves through a series of keys without establishing any of them.

The same alternation of solo and tutti that defines the overall form also serves important structural functions within the first solo. In particular, textural contrast articulates the modulation to the dominant key. A "brief interruption from the orchestra, *forte*," precedes that modulation (though it may also be perceived as providing dynamic reinforcement to the tonic close of the first theme group), and another follows the modulation in order to confirm the new key.[6] The solo writing meanwhile climaxes in "cadential virtuosity, the scales, flourishes, and trills that mark the end of a solo section."

While the end of the sonata exposition is usually articulated by a rest, in the concerto the solo exposition leads directly into the second ritornello. (In fact, the solo characteristically ends with a trill whose resolution coincides with the onset of the ritornello, thus guaranteeing continuity.) Rosen investigates the nature of this second ritornello in terms of its "sonata" function, considering first whether its opening constitutes the ending of the exposition or the beginning of the development. The latter impression is created if the ritornello starts with the first theme in the dominant (a choice representing the earlier concerto tradition), for this suggests a new beginning and is an option commonly found in sonata developments. On the other hand, if it starts with the closing themes of the first ritornello (the more modern choice, which Rosen claims was "developed in the 1760s"), it takes on the character of an ending – specifically, the ending of the exposition. However, though the ritornello often ends with a strong cadence in the dominant, it need not do so. Instead, it may lead into the third solo and thus contain the beginning of the development as well as the end of the exposition. In such cases, Rosen describes the second ritornello as a "transition between two solo sections, end and new beginning at one and the same time."

By analogy with the sonata development, the second solo may begin with the first theme in the dominant or with a "new" theme "of expressive character." Even if themes are not actually "developed," the "texture" is that of a development, with "fragmentation, sequential harmony, wide-ranging modulation," and "fast-moving harmonic rhythm." There may also be "a good deal of rhapsodic arpeggiation" on the part of the soloist: a figurational style suggestive of improvisation and therefore ideally suited to the concerto. Rosen cites Beethoven's First and Fifth Piano Concertos, but Mozart's in G Major, K. 453, also comes to mind.

The balance of the concerto movement receives relatively short shrift. Rosen notes the common practice of combining the third ritornello and third solo, and relates this to his observation that the third solo is the one most frequently interrupted by the orchestra. He also describes Mozart's occasional practice of including in the third solo a ritornello theme that had been omitted from the solo exposition. These points all support Tovey's view that the concerto recapitulation is of both the orchestral and solo expositions.

Rosen's discussion of the Classical concerto and its conventions in *Sonata Forms* is thus much richer in descriptive detail than his earlier account, but he has not altered his essential analytical stance, articulated in *The Classical Style*. There he argued against the notion "that there was such a thing as 'sonata form' in the late eighteenth century, and that composers knew what it was." He conceded that particular "patterns" and devices were "most commonly used" as they were "the easiest and most effective ways of meeting the demands the public made of the composer or, rather, that he made upon himself. But these patterns were not the form, and they only became so when the creative impulse and the style that generated the form had almost completely died away." In his view, then, it is necessary to appreciate the full range of options and possibilities within the style in order to "distinguish what is abnormal only in a statistical sense from what was genuinely astonishing." This is a crucial distinction, but to a large degree it is a judgment made by the individual listener, based on that individual's experience, expectations, and, above all, knowledge of conventions. It should also be noted that while Rosen rejects a definition of form *in terms of* the conventions, his own hearing of works (and consequently of their forms) is dependent on his own highly developed and well-informed awareness of the conventions, which is ultimately what enables him to distinguish the normative from the abnormal and the abnormal from the astonishing.

A detailed, even statistical, knowledge of the conventions of the Classical concerto is thus highly desirable regardless of one's analytical stance with respect to musical form. To invoke the dichotomy and definitions proposed by Mark Evan Bonds, such knowledge is obviously basic to the "conformational" approach, which compares each "specific work against an abstract, ideal type," but it is just as relevant, albeit in a different way, to the "generative" approach of Tovey and Rosen, which "considers how each individual work grows from within and how the various elements of a work coordinate to make a coherent whole" (Bonds, pp. 13–14).

Daniel Leeson & Robert Levin

The kind of comprehensive statistical survey of Classical concerto form (or at least of first-movement form) that might answer the needs of both analytical orientations – the "generative" and the "conformational" – was undertaken by Daniel N. Leeson and Robert D. Levin in connection with their article "On the Authenticity of K. Anh. C14.01 (297b), a Symphonia Concertante for Four Winds and Orchestra," published in the *Mozart-Jahrbuch 1976/77*. In an effort to develop an objective methodology for testing the authenticity of the extant score of Mozart's Symphonie Concertante for Winds, Leeson and Levin focused on its first movement (because Mozart used a variety of forms for his slow movements and finales, but the same form for first movements), which they compared with the opening movements of Mozart's thirty-nine authentic concertos (and *symphonies concertantes*), using as a "control repertoire" concertos and *symphonies concertantes* by prominent contemporaries: J. C. Bach, Boccherini, Dittersdorf, Joseph Haydn, Karl Stamitz, Viotti, and Vogler.[7] Among other things, Leeson and Levin concluded that "there is a simple, unchanging, general scheme to the opening movements of all Mozart's works for solo instrument(s) and orchestra"; that "this scheme has three consistent factors: a) the proportions which prevail between the structural sections of each movement; b) the thematic patterns within each section; and c) the thematic coherence between sections"; and that "within reasonable statistical limits, the scheme is constant throughout Mozart's life" and is, moreover, "unique to Mozart." These were the conclusions needed for their immediate purpose, which was to discover "objective" criteria against which to measure the work of questionable authenticity.

Of course, this is not the only use to which the Leeson–Levin "Thematic/Structural Model" might be put. In fact, this particular statistical approach to the concertos was originally stimulated by an entirely different project: Levin's completions of a special class of Mozart fragments – movement beginnings that Mozart set aside and probably intended to finish but never did, presumably because the need for the completed compositions failed to materialize. To provide a model for his completion of the fragmentary Concerto in D Major for Piano, Violin, and Orchestra, K. Anh. 56/315f, he undertook a structural study of Mozart's concertos, concentrating on the period before November 1778, when the fragment was presumably drafted. This study yielded the prototype for the later, more developed Leeson–Levin model.[8] This context helps to explain why Leeson and Levin located their "norm" in the concertos of Mozart's early maturity, whereas Tovey, with his unabashed elitism, turned for his model to a "late" masterpiece (K. 503), and Rosen, with a comparable esteem for "genius" but interested in seeking out the exceptional in order to isolate the genre's essential "lowest common denominators," took as his point of departure in *The Classical Style* the atypical and even quirky K. 271.

As admirable as it is in many respects, the Leeson–Levin model raises certain problems for our present purpose, which is to identify the conventions of the Classical concerto and so determine the expectations a contemporary listener might have brought to hearing a Mozart concerto. Levin and Leeson's specific research projects needed a model both to guide the completion of concerto fragments and to serve as a yardstick against which to test a work of dubious authenticity. As a result they focused of necessity on Mozart's individual, even idiosyncratic, practices to the exclusion of other, possibly even more widespread, conventions and alternatives. The Leeson–Levin model thus presents analysts, both "conformational" and "generative," with a perspective and touchstone that are purely and uniquely Mozartian. If there were eighteenth-century listeners who had anything like it in mind, they had to have been true and devoted connoisseurs of Mozart's concerto output. Such listeners would have constituted a rather exclusive group, probably limited to the composer and his immediate circle of family and pupils.

A similar limitation applies to an earlier statistical survey, Hans Tischler's *A Structural Analysis of Mozart's Piano Concertos* (1966), a collection of thematic, structural, and tonal diagrams of the original piano concerto movements, supplemented by statistical summaries of Mozart's structural choices. Even more than Leeson–Levin, Tischler's collection of data dramatizes the need for a rapprochement between the "conformational" and "generative" perspectives. As Bonds observed: "Both [the generative and conformational] approaches are valid, yet neither is sufficient for musical analysis. Looking for stereotypical patterns can help call attention to deviations from a recognized norm, but it cannot explain these deviations. At the same time, analyzing a work entirely 'from within' cannot account for the striking structural similarities that exist among a large number of quite independent works" (p. 14). With this in mind, the following presentation of the Leeson–Levin model will simultaneously seek to understand it from a "generative" point of view, insofar as this is possible in the abstract.

Leeson–Levin divides the Mozart concerto first movement into seven sections, but the divisions differ somewhat from the seven identified by Rosen as normative for the mid-century "son-of-Bach" concerto. In Leeson–Levin, the seven sections are: (1) opening ritornello, (2) solo exposition, (3) middle ritornello, (4) development, (5) recapitulation, (6) ritornello to cadenza, and (7) final ritornello. (The solo cadenza is an implicit eighth section preceding the final ritornello.) As might be expected from this mixture of concerto and sonata labels, the section divisions are not defined strictly according to the alternation of tutti and solo textures. Notably, sections 4 and 5, which bear consecutive sonata-form labels (development and recapitulation), are not texturally identified, although both are implicitly solo dominated. Characteristically, however, there is some tutti articulation at this juncture, but it is often very short, and it can occur at different points within the sonata structure. Most often a tutti marks the beginning of the recapitulation (as the Rosen diagram implies and as occurs in K. 466 and K. 467, among many other examples), but there are instances in which it either articulates the end of the development (K. 271, K. 413, and K. 459) or constitutes both the end of the development and beginning of the recapitulation (K. 453 and 456). In K. 415 there is no intervening tutti at all, as the solo plays almost continually throughout the development and begins the recapitulation as well. This variety of options may have motivated Leeson–Levin to focus on the "invariant" sonata elements as section-defining, though the first option listed above (a tutti beginning the recapitulation) is statistically most common and apparently "normative."

Leeson–Levin divides the **opening ritornello** into seven thematic/structural events numbered *1–7* and organized, like a sonata exposition, into primary and secondary groups. Also part of the scheme is a particular pattern of dynamic contrast, not surprising for a genre defined by its contrast of unequal forces:[9]

(*1*) The "first theme," which culminates in a perfect cadence in the tonic, is usually soft but might also exhibit a loud–soft pattern.

(*2*) The "forte move to the dominant [chord]" which follows is "more active" and is directed toward:

(*3*) A half-cadence on (not "in") the dominant. Together, these three elements constitute the "primary group" of the opening ritornello, analogous to the "primary group" of a sonata exposition, with *1* corresponding to the first theme or group of themes and *2* and *3* together resembling a bridge. Since the "bridge" in this case culminates in the dominant chord of the home tonic, it may suggest but does not effect a modulation. However, a parallel may be found in a particular type of sonata form in which the medial cadence (at the end of the bridge) is likewise a half-cadence on the dominant, followed in the exposition by the second theme *in* the dominant (treating the dominant chord of the half-cadence as a *tonic chord* in the *dominant key*), and in the recapitulation by the second theme in the *tonic* (resolving the dominant chord of the half-cadence "properly"). Nearly 150 examples of this gambit may be found among Mozart's sonata-form movements, and in the first movements of the Piano Concertos K. 413/387a and K. 482 he exploits the tonal ambiguity of this gesture in strikingly different ways.[10]

(4) A "more lyric" soft theme in the tonic begins the secondary group. It resembles the second theme of a sonata, and that tends to be its destiny in the solo expositions of Mozart's early concertos (before 1779). In later concertos the solo expositions will often present different second themes, moving Girdlestone in such cases to call the ritornello lyric theme a " 'mock' second subject"; Levin has similarly labeled it a "false second theme."[11] Such characterizations suggest that Mozart sought to thwart our expectations, surprising us in the solo exposition with the arrival of the "real" second theme. It may be more useful to view it as a theme which the orchestra proposes as a candidate for the position of exposition second theme, which the solo is free to accept or reject – or which the orchestra might impose. Exceptionally, in the first movement of the Piano Concerto in E-flat Major, K. 449 (1784), the ritornello lyric theme is in the dominant, having been preceded by an actual modulation, with the *forte* half-cadence being *in* the dominant key; this lyric theme is then followed by another, never heard from again, which restores the tonic key.[12]

(5) The first concluding motive, which is *forte*, may be analogous in its "energy" to 2, but it leads to a perfect cadence in the tonic.

(6) There is often a second concluding motive, also cadencing in the tonic, but it tends to be *piano* and "less assertive."

(7) A "brief flourish" in the tonic, *forte*, concludes the secondary group and the ritornello.

The secondary group, like the primary, has obvious correspondences to a sonata exposition, in this case to the second- and closing-theme areas, though of course all ritornello themes are typically in the tonic key. The abundance of closing themes is desirable given the need for a fairly substantial final ritornello following the cadenza and the Mozartian principle of thematic economy, whereby subsequent ritornellos derive their materials entirely from the opening ritornello.

In mapping out the balance of the first movement, Leeson–Levin uses capital letters to identify themes or motives originating in the solo sections, in order to distinguish them from materials derived from the ritornellos, which are numbered. Variants of previously labeled materials are signaled by a prime (e.g., A' would be a variant of A). "Supplementary material" is labeled with Roman numerals when introduced by the orchestra, and with lowercase letters when introduced by the solo. The Leeson–Levin model allows for such a "supplementary section" immediately preceding the exposition, labeled "I/a" because it is "a supplementary section begun by the orchestra that is used to introduce the soloist." The section is considered supplementary in the sense that it does not replace any portion of the solo exposition. As examples, Levin points to the Piano Concertos K. 467 and K. 503, in which "the orchestra seems to coax the soloist into entering," and the Piano Concerto K. 271 and the Sinfonia Concertante for Violin and Viola K. 364/320d, in which "the soloist surprises us by entering over the waning measures of the opening ritornello."[13] Such solo entrances sometimes conclude in an *Eingang* or lead -in, either written out or improvised.

The **solo exposition**, according to the Leeson–Levin model, characteristically begins with the soloist playing the first theme (*1*), frequently followed by the ritornello "flourish" (*7*) played by the orchestra. Having just provided closure to the ritornello, the flourish here reinforces and confirms the cadence and tonality of the first theme, thus "freeing the soloist to modulate." In his mature piano concertos Mozart tended either simply to omit the flourish, to replace it with a different concluding theme (e.g., *5* in K. 537), to insert instead the *forte* drive to V (*2*) to initiate the motion to the dominant (e.g., K. 451, K. 453, K. 456, K. 488), or else to use an entirely different mechanism for both introducing the solo and responding with orchestral confirmation of the tonic. This alternative opening gambit, which Levin finds in the Piano Concertos K. 466, K. 482, and K. 491 among others, has the solo introduce a new theme ("always [having] a definite improvisatory quality") "as an addition to the form," after which delay the orchestra supplies the (expected?) opening theme (*1*), perhaps with solo participation.[14] This alternative opening, like the "supplementary section" described above, is a trenchant way to introduce the soloist, spotlighting its distinct and independent character – especially effective, and in some cases even necessary, when the opening theme of the ritornello is not readily adaptable to solo performance. Of course, there need not be the exigency of an "un-pianistic" first theme for Mozart to choose such a non-normative solo entry, as in the case of the Piano Concerto K. 450, where the soloist enters with new material and then takes up the first theme. One thing is certain: Mozart would not have begun a piano concerto with an "unpianistic" first theme without having anticipated the consequences and possibilities, especially for the solo exposition and recapitulation.

The next events in the Leeson–Levin exposition model are a new theme (A) played by the solo, which modulates to the dominant key (or the relative major, in a minor-key concerto) and concludes on the threshold of that key with a half-cadence played by the orchestra, using either 3 from the ritornello or new cadential material (B). Although these themes are ostensibly comparable to the "bridge" or "transition" of a sonata exposition, Levin borrows the term *sujet libre* (from Saint-Foix) to describe A, defining it as a theme "which often does not reappear in the recapitulation, but serves as a harmonic catalyst in moving the piece from the tonic to [the dominant:] V or V of V."[15] For Leeson–Levin this concludes the primary group of the solo exposition and would seem to be appropriate and sufficient preparation for the secondary group in the new key.

What typically follows, however, is not the expected second theme, but an episode (C), played by the solo, which lacks the "tonal stability" of the new key and thus "has the character of introducing the new tonality rather than asserting it." The orchestra concludes this episode with another half-cadence (less commonly, a perfect cadence) in the new key, using either 3, if it had not been used for the previous half-cadence, or a new theme (B or BB). By using two distinct themes to accomplish the modulation – the *sujet libre* (A) and the episode (C), both articulated by orchestral (half-) cadences – Mozart effectively "thematizes" the transition and highlights the solo's role as the modulatory agent. In some of the later piano concertos, the modulation is achieved via an intermediary tonality introduced in episode C – the dominant minor in K. 467, K. 482, and K. 595, and the flat mediant in K. 503. This intermediary tonality suggests the so-called "three-key exposition," associated with such later composers as Schubert, Brahms, and Bruckner, but relatively uncommon in the eighteenth century.[16]

Having accomplished the modulation to the dominant key (or the relative major in a minor-key movement), the solo typically begins the secondary group either with the ritornello lyric theme (4) or, more commonly after 1778, with a new theme (*D*). Occasionally the orchestra introduces this second theme, particularly when it is *4*, its own ritornello theme, but it may also inaugurate a new theme, as happens in K. 459. In such cases the solo will soon join in and will probably co-opt the theme. The second theme culminates in a cadence in the dominant key and is followed by a coda (*E*), typically virtuosic in character. As Joseph Kerman observed, in the "two solo spans," the solo exposition and recapitulation, the solo "traverses a broad trajectory from discourse to display."[17] *E* is the culmination of that trajectory, and it climaxes in a cadential trill, signaling the close of the solo exposition. While *E* usually consists of new material, it may incorporate themes from the ritornello closing, especially *5* or *6*.

The full orchestra enters *forte* on the resolution of the solo's cadential trill with the **middle ritornello**. Tovey derived its function from the "concerto principle": that whenever the solo marks an important harmonic arrival by climaxing in a key, the orchestra enters in that key with parts of its opening ritornello to supply the missing element of sonic force. That being the case, the primary thematic candidates to launch the middle ritornello are the *forte* themes from the opening ritornello: *2* or *5*, leading to a cadence in the dominant key. In a few instances, Mozart begins instead with new material or a variant of the opening theme. The latter option, exercised in the Flute Concerto K. 313/285c and the Piano Concertos K. 415/387b and K. 459, seems to hark back to an earlier style of concerto form, in which this ritornello functioned as an independent section with a new beginning rather than as an orchestral closing appended to the solo exposition.[18] Indeed, the themes for the middle ritornello seem chosen not simply for their *forte* dynamic, but because they are cadence-directed and, in comparison with the often extended virtuosic drive that closes the solo exposition, are more likely to be constructed of short, repeating cadential phrases. In other words, the middle ritornello themes more closely resemble the closing theme(s) of a sonata exposition. (Rosen, it will be recalled, labeled this section the "cadential tutti" and conceived it as part of the "exposition.") The closing function of the middle ritornello is reinforced by Mozart's tendency also to use other concluding themes from the opening ritornello: *6* and *7*. In a few cases (e.g., K. 459, K. 467, and K. 595) the middle ritornello does not end with a cadence in the dominant, but modulates to usher in the development in a new key.

The **development** is implicitly a solo section and follows no pre-scribed plan. Like a sonata development it may offer non-thematic "improvisatory" passagework, introduce new themes, or utilize material previously heard.

In labeling the next section **recapitulation** and discussing it without reference to texture and purely in terms of thematic and harmonic design, Leeson–Levin is clearly privileging the sonata perspective – and with good reason. Nevertheless, the frequent presence of a tutti passage at the juncture of development and recapitulation is hardly the vestigial and anachronistic legacy of an earlier concerto practice (recall *R3* from Rosen's diagram of the mid-eighteenth-century concerto). Rather, it is an important feature of concerto design that supports Tovey's view that the recapitulation is of both the opening ritornello and the solo exposi-tion, integrating both textural and thematic elements. Symbolically, this point can be instantly and effectively made at the outset of the recapitula-tion by beginning with the opening ritornello theme played by the orchestra alone and then having the solo join in after just a few bars, as happens more often than not in Mozart's piano concertos.[19] This common procedure is perhaps a refinement of the strategy employed in the Piano Concerto K. 175 (1773) and the Bassoon Concerto K. 191/186e (1774), Mozart's earliest surviving "original" concertos, in which the orchestra plays the first few bars of the first theme (three bars in the piano concerto, four in that for bassoon), after which the entire theme is played by the soloist. In the Piano Concerto K. 453, the tutti begins with a two-bar orchestral lead-in from the development and is fairly substantial – a further thirty bars, but with the piano participating in six of these, starting eight bars in. An alternative strategy, found in the Piano Concerto K. 451, has the piano play continuously during the first fifteen bars of the recapitulation, but its contributions are largely deco-rative, superimposed on an essentially self-sufficient orchestral presentation of the opening themes. A tutti function is thereby sug-gested, even without a textural break and despite the striking solo pres-ence. There are admittedly instances where the development and recapitulation are texturally more or less continuous, without significant tutti articulation, as in the Piano Concerto K. 415/387b, where the solo leads into and begins the recapitulation. In the Piano Concertos K. 413/387a and K. 459, a short tutti (of three and six bars, respectively) ends the development, after which the solo begins the recapitulation. Each of the various textural options available at this structural point reflects a different relationship between solo and orchestra. The scoring of the recapitulation is thus always of more than incidental interest, as the effect of the form cannot be fully appreciated from a thematic chart alone.

Normatively, the recapitulation begins with the ritornello's first theme (*1*) introduced by the orchestra, even when the solo exposition had been inaugurated by a new solo theme or "supplementary section" (e.g., K. 271, K. 450, K. 466, K. 467, K. 482, K. 491, and K. 503). Leeson–Levin notes that Mozart tends to carry out the recapitulation somewhat differently at different stages in his career. In the early concertos he typically follows the thematic sequence of the exposition, merely introducing the necessary harmonic adjustments in the episode and secondary group to retain the tonic key. In the later works, however, he tends to streamline or modify the primary group in its path to the orchestral half-cadence in the tonic (*3* or *B*): the flourish (*7* or its replacement) is omitted, and the *sujet libre* (*A*) might be transformed, replaced by an extension of the first theme, or even cut altogether. In essence, elements associated with the exposition's modulation are suppressed or played down, sometimes in favor of the corresponding portions of the ritornello, whose harmonic stability is more in keeping with the tonal destiny of the recapitulation. Thus in the later concertos the recapitulation characteristically begins by tracing the thematic sequence of the ritornello, albeit with solo participation, sometimes even as far as the half-cadence in the tonic (*3*, as in K. 453), or exceptionally even beyond, through the ritornello lyric theme (*4*, as in K. 482). The balance of the recapitulation, however, must include the tonic resolution of the exposition's secondary group and therefore tends to pick up the thematic sequence of the solo exposition, making the necessary tonal adjustments: the episode (*C*), half-cadence (*3*, *B* or *BB*), and the secondary group (*D* and/or *4*, then *E*). Of course, there are exceptional instances where ritornello and exposition materials mix in ways perhaps unanticipated. Notably when the solo exposition has introduced a new second theme (*D*) in preference to the ritornello second theme (*4*), the latter might return as an interpolation in the coda (e.g., K. 450, K. 467, K. 491, and K 503) or even precede the "new" second theme (e.g., K. 482). On the other hand, when the solo exposition offers both second themes, the recapitulation tends to follow suit.

In combining aspects of both ritornello and exposition, the recapitulation thus offers an almost labyrinthine array of options, particularly in the later concertos, whose expositions tend to introduce "new" first and second themes. Though certain normative patterns do emerge, it is no wonder that Tovey chose to emphasize the capacity of Mozart's recapitulations to surprise, despite the logic of their designs: "There is no foreseeing what the solo will select from the ritornello. All that we can be sure of is that nothing will be without its function, and that everything will be unexpected and inevitable."

Like the middle ritornello, the **ritornello to the cadenza** typically begins with the full orchestra entering *forte* on the resolution of the solo's cadential trill. It culminates, however, not in a perfect cadence, but on a cadential six-four chord, thus inviting the solo cadenza. This ritornello is relatively short. It consists most often of a single theme, though sometimes there are two, and rarely even three. The principal thematic possibilities are the same as were candidates for the middle ritornello, i.e., the *forte* themes from the opening ritornello: most frequently, the *forte* move to V (*2*) and, less often, the first concluding theme (*5*) or a variant of the opening theme (*1'*). In a few cases the cadenza is approached by *3*, the half-cadence motive from the ritornello. In his mature piano concertos of 1784–6, Mozart characteristically uses the same theme to begin both the middle ritornello and the ritornello to the cadenza, thus creating a thematic symmetry between the tutti passages that "close" the exposition and the recapitulation. In his earlier concertos, such thematic symmetry far more commonly links the middle ritornello with the final ritornello.

Like its predecessors, the **final ritornello**, following the cadenza, generally starts *forte* with the orchestral re-entry on the tonic resolution of the solo's cadential trill. Its thematic materials are drawn chiefly from the concluding themes of the opening ritornello, thereby creating a symmetry between the two ritornellos that frame the movement and possibly with the middle ritornello as well, since it too may contain the same sequence of themes. The final ritornello begins most often with *5*, the first, *forte* concluding theme. Alternatively, *2*, the *forte* move to V, may be used, provided it has not already appeared in the preceding ritornello to the cadenza. (Mozart almost never uses the same theme in *both* of these last two ritornellos, though there are exceptions, such as the Piano Concertos K. 238 and K. 450 and the Flute Concerto K. 314/285d.) A "special" effect is produced in the Piano Concertos K. 451 and K. 453 by beginning the final ritornello with 6, the second, *piano* concluding theme, producing a relatively "hushed" orchestral response to the cadenza. 6 and/or 7 typically conclude the final ritornello, though they are sometimes followed by an extension (*8*), which differentiates it from the opening ritornello and produces greater finality. Exceptionally, in the Piano Concertos K. 271 and K. 491 this extension is substantial and the soloist joins in.

In the following chapters the diagrammatic representations of the individual concerto movements are intended to illustrate large-scale form, and the labeling system is geared toward thematic function rather than motivic relationships. Efforts (like Tischler's) to do justice to such relationships invariably require complex, even bewildering systems of symbols, with Arabic and Roman numbers, upper- and lowercase letters, and an assortment of sub- and superscripts. The results are often harder to read than a score – and far less illuminating. The labeling system used below to represent the concerto first and middle movements is considerably simpler and is essentially that of the Leeson–Levin model. I find such diagrams useful, but their utility to the listener is debatable. Virgil Thomson, in an epistolary critique of Aaron Copland's *What to Listen for in Music* (1939), questioned the virtue and even the possibility of "analytic listening" and suggested that listeners might "just as well . . . let themselves follow the emotional line of a piece."[20] The narrative accounts of the concertos that follow will, I hope, also offer insight into their "emotional lines," as will great performances of them. All too often, when a performance is praised for its analytical acuity, "intelligence," or knowing projection of the musical "architecture" (the auditory equivalent of a diagram?), it turns out to mean little more than that continuity has been sustained, but at the expense of "character" and by minimizing a sense of discrete musical "events." To my way of thinking, this is no great accomplishment. It does not serve the music as I understand it, for without sensitivity to the musical "event" we will surely miss the "special moments" that make the concertos so treasurable.[21]

3

First movements

K. 466: Allegro

In the typical mixed concert of the late eighteenth century, the concerto's usual position, somewhere in the middle of the program, meant that it was under less pressure to grab the audience's attention with a loud beginning than was the symphony, which was likely to open the concert. But such programming considerations are just one of the reasons why Mozart's concertos tend to begin *piano*, whereas his symphonies usually start *forte*. Another practical reason stems from the normative formal strategy of the concerto first movement, which calls for the same theme to open both the orchestral ritornello and the solo exposition: if that theme is soft, the solo instrument (in particular, Mozart's fortepiano, but other potential solo instruments as well) stands a better chance of giving as effective an account of that theme as the orchestra had, and thus of establishing itself as an equal to the large ensemble.

The opening of the first movement of the D-minor Concerto is indeed marked *piano*; but the foreboding syncopated string chords, combined with the menacing rising "slide" figure in the cellos and basses, is more an ominous pulsation than a conventional melody. This syncopated minor-key opening may call to mind Mozart's "Little" G-minor Symphony, K. 183/173dB, but there is an important difference. The symphony's syncopations, *forte* and contained within the bar, place us in the presence of some frightening apparition – as in *Don Giovanni* – while in the concerto the terror is still unknown. Inherently orchestral, this opening texture does not translate well into pianistic terms. Thus, from the moment he conceived it, Mozart must have foreseen the solo entering with something entirely different. Unable to adopt the theme, the solo will be forced to confront it. (Mozart's two-stave reduction of the

31

theme as an incipit in his autograph thematic catalogue is ineffective as piano music, while Beethoven's thrilling "translation" of it in his magnificent cadenza for the movement only proves that one must exceed the limits of Mozart's keyboard style to achieve such an effect.) K. 467 begins with a very different theme but nonetheless presents a similar situation. There the orchestra's unison theme would likewise seem to disallow effective presentation by the solo, despite its contrapuntal potential. The orchestral opening of K. 466 is all the more striking when one considers that the four piano concertos that immediately preceded it – K. 451, K. 453, K. 456, and K. 459 – all began with precisely the same rhythmic motive (♩ ♪♩. ♪) and, in three of the four, on repetitions of the same pitch.

In K. 466, the scoring of the opening is subtle and miraculous, with the wind pairs stealthily joining the strings, one at a time, averting an effect of a sonic accumulation. The *forte* explosion with which the entire orchestra bursts in at bar 16 thus delivers the shock of a thunderclap. If what follows is heard as a *forte* restatement of the opening theme (a strategy also encountered in the surrounding Piano Concertos, K. 459 and K. 467, as well as in K. 491), it is, as Charles Rosen points out, of necessity "radically transformed," and "into something very like Don Giovanni's duel with the Commendatore."[1] Messiaen, emphasizing the bold downward arpeggios rather than the rising, swashbuckling bass figure, compared this moment to the Et incarnatus est from Bach's B-minor Mass and the oracle's pronouncement in Act I of Gluck's *Alceste*.[2] We may also hear in it an anticipation of the Queen of the Night's Act II aria. (Why some such transformation would be necessary is immediately apparent the moment one tries to imagine the initial theme played loudly.) In the Leeson–Levin scheme this corresponds to the "*forte* move to the dominant" (Fig. 1: *2*), though the energy is so powerful that the harmonic gesture is made twice. The first (*2A*), ending in a half-cadence at bars 21–3, is insufficient in length or force to dissipate the mounting "charge," so a second approach to the dominant follows (*2B*), reverting to syncopated material and a *piano* dynamic before culminating in a longer and more emphatic *forte* half-cadence (Fig. 1: *3*, bars 28–32), hammered home in dotted rhythms and followed by a dramatic caesura.

Out of this dramatic pause, a soft lyric theme emerges in the winds (Fig. 1: *4*, bars 33–43) – the orchestra's "second-theme" candidate.

While bringing momentary relief, it proves to be problematic, its nature and status complicated by the movement's minor modality. While Mozart's typical ritornello holds throughout to the tonic key, this theme begins on a harmonic *non sequitur*, apparently in the relative major (F major). It thus seems to anticipate the key to which the solo exposition will modulate – the very key in which it would return in that section, were that to be its destiny. Such a strategy would not be unthinkable, as Mozart earlier demonstrated (not without telling twists) in the Piano Concertos in F, K. 413/387a, and E-flat, K. 449, but it is not what happens here. This turns out not to be a stable, balanced theme, nor is it able to sustain the relative major. While its F-major beginning suggests a potential for relief from the oppressive minor modality, its harmonically restless sequential repetitions prevent it from achieving that goal, and it is pulled down to D minor – the key which, we realize, it has never really left. This lyric theme is thus unsuited to serve as the "second theme" of the solo exposition, unless it were to undergo radical transformation. In setting the principal terms of the movement, Mozart has devised a ritornello that will virtually require the solo to introduce independent material for both its first and second themes. A dynamic relationship with the orchestra is thus preordained.

The closing themes reclaim D minor with a vengeance and sustain the remarkable passion and homogeneity of the ritornello, with tremolo textures, tonic pedals, chromatic neighbor motion, appoggiaturas, syncopations, and dramatic downward arpeggios echoing prior themes. Instead of the stereotypical Leeson–Levin pattern of two closing themes and a flourish, dynamically differentiated by a *forte–piano–forte* pattern, we find a long sustained *forte* theme of 27 bars (Fig. 1: 5) that twice feigns dynamic softening before finally easing into the six-bar *piano* theme that closes the ritornello in a state of quiet despair (Fig. 1: 6) – the lull in the storm that gives the solo reason to emerge. Clearly, a celebratory flourish is out of the question. The lengthy *forte* closing theme (Fig. 1: 5) is prolonged by internal repetitions and may be mapped as *abb–a'cc'*. Its essential two–part structure will have ramifications for the solo "codas" of the exposition and recapitulation, and when it returns in the final ritornello, following the cadenza, the repetitions will be shorn and the theme thereby condensed to its essence: *ab–a'c'*. The *piano* close of the opening ritornello establishes a pattern of hushed endings that will be emulated

Figure 1 *K. 466/1, organization*

RITORNELLO

R1 (76 bars)

bar	1	16	28	33		44	71
theme	*1*	*2*	*3*	*4*		*5*	*6*
key	d						

EXPOSITION

S1 (97 bars) *R2* (18 bars)

bar	77	91	108	115	127	143	153	174	186
theme	*N*	*1*	*3*	*4*	*D*	*E*	*5'*	*2*	*6*
key	d				F			F	

DEVELOPMENT

S2 (62 bars)

bar	192	202	206	216	220	232	236	240	250
theme	*N*	*1*	*N*	*1*	*N*	*1*	*1*	*1*	*2'*
key	F		g	Eb $\to$ f $\to$		g $\to$ V/d			

RECAPITULATION

R3 S3 (7 bars + 95 bars) *R4* (10+32 = 42 bars)

bar	254	261	269	281	288	302	318	330	356	365	366	384	390	394
theme	*1*	*2*	*3*	*4*	*D*	*E*	*5'*	*2A*	cadenza		*5*	*6*	*1'*	& *2'*
key	d													
	≈*R1*		≈*S1*						≈*R2*		≈*R1*		= NEW	

Tutti themes are shown in boldface. The horizontal spacing between themes does not necessarily reflect their relative lengths; they are aligned vertically with their recurrences in subsequent sections.

in the succeeding ritornellos, both following the solo exposition and at the end of the movement.

Ending the opening ritornello *piano* – or in Leeson–Levin terms, suppressing the expected concluding *forte* flourish – is not without precedent in Mozart's piano concertos, but it is an unusual choice, and when adopted in the Piano Concertos K. 413 and K. 450 it was in conjunction with a solo entrance that not only introduced a new theme, but overlapped with the close of the ritornello. In K. 466 the soloist begins with a new theme (labeled *N*, for "new"), but without the overlap. Ellwood Derr has argued that the "new" themes with which Mozart introduces the soloist in the solo expositions of nine of his piano concerto first movements (K. 271, K. 413/387a, K. 415/387b, K. 450, K. 466, K. 467, K. 482, K. 491, and K. 503) are analogous to the *fermata sospesa*, the singer's generally unmeasured elaboration, after the opening ritornello, on the first word of the aria text.[3] This intriguing suggestion is not particularly convincing in relation to K. 466, where the solo theme not only has a "composed" rather than improvised character, but is integral to the argument of the movement. It figures prominently in the second solo (the development) and, as Charles Rosen has observed, belongs to a family of themes whose relatedness contributes to the homogeneity of the movement and offers a link to the finale.[4] Its connection to the ritornello lyric theme (Fig. 1: *4*) is most immediately germane, as the solo now gives voice to the longing for relief promised, but not delivered, in the ritornello. The expressive, highly personal quality of this utterance is enhanced by virtue of the fact that this unaccompanied solo theme is thus far the most regular, balanced, and "vocal."

(A note to pianists: In his 1827 edition of K. 466, Johann Nepomuk Hummel, a Mozart pupil, wrote out the execution of the ornamental appoggiatura in the third beat of bar 87 according to the time-honored principle that it last two-thirds the value of the dotted main note, and that the short note following the main note be shortened, precisely as Leopold Mozart recommended in his *Violinschule*, ch. 9, section 4 (see Example 1). Frederick Neumann has argued that Mozart only rarely adhered to the "two-thirds rule,"[5] yet Hummel's realization, which may reflect how he might have heard Mozart play the passage, enhances the expressive quality of the appoggiatura and emphasizes its motivic significance.)

Apparently unmoved by the piano's plea, the strings reassert their

Example 1 K. 466/I, with Hummel's realization of appoggiatura

original syncopated theme (Fig. 1: *1*). After four bars, however, the piano joins in, initially tracing the string parts but soon taking the lead, neutralizing the orchestra's syncopations and with its continuous right-hand figuration giving the music a more agitated character. Under the stress of the solo presence, the first violins become more chromatic and less sustained, and the winds hesitate before entering. After twice threatening to do so, the piano finally breaks free of theme *1* in bar 104 and in a flurry of activity proceeds to the ritornello theme that had marked the half-cadence (Fig. 1: *3*), which is now extended from five to seven bars and proceeds in three distinct orchestrational blocks, passing by increments from solo to tutti: solo piano, piano and winds, and finally the full orchestra alone. The exposition opening has thus established a dialogue between solo and orchestra through the opposition of their independent "first" themes. The solo, however, co-opts the orchestra's theme *1*, directing it not to a perfect cadence but to a half-cadence, thus forcing it to assume the function of its transformed *forte* counterstatement (theme *2* of the ritornello) in leading to theme *3*.

The texture having been returned to the orchestra, the exposition continues the prior sequence of ritornello themes with the lyric theme *4*. The piano initially cooperates in the presentation of this theme, adopting the flute part to engage in dialogue with the winds, but beginning in bar 121 it replaces the "background" oboe suspensions with a distinctive melodic line that moves it into the foreground as the apparent active agent responsible for breaking the sequence pattern and redirecting the tonality "back" to F major, the relative major and the expected key of the exposition second group. With the energy generated by its increased rhythmic activity, the solo leads to a half-cadence in the new key followed by a caesura.

The motivic connections among the themes have profound dramatic significance. The solo, having identified (through *N*) with the aspirations of the thwarted ritornello lyric theme (*4*), helps it realize its potential, first by enabling its exposition version to complete the promised path to major-key relief and then, through the same motivic link, by transforming it into the exposition "second theme" in F major (Fig. 1:*D*, in bar 127). The first phrase of *D* is unaccompanied, an acknowledgement of the solo's crucial role in securing the modulation, but its second is warmly received by the strings, signifying orchestral acquiescence. The F-minor inflections of the preceding half-cadence only enhance the freshness of the arrival by providing a local element of minor–major contrast to make palpable the modal shift that is operating on the larger, structural level. The balanced symmetry of this new theme contrasts markedly with everything that has been heard so far and offers a ready vehicle for dialogue among the three main sonorous agents – piano, strings, and winds.

At its concluding cadence, the piano launches the exposition "coda" theme (Fig. 1: *E*, at bar 143), marked, as is the norm, by athletic energy and bravura passagework, culminating in the so-called "piano climax," the cadential trill on the supertonic that signals the re-entry of the orchestra for the middle ritornello. This trill arrives prematurely, after only ten bars, suggesting a victory too easily won. A memory, however, seems to be triggered by the rising chromaticism of the immediately preceding broken-octave scale (bar 151) – of a ritornello theme that shares this figure and is also a candidate for "redemption": the *forte* closing theme (*5*). This theme is thus subsumed in the final dash to closure, its two-part structure still manifest: a section derived from its first part (bars 44ff) leads to the second cadential trill, and a section based on its second part (bars 58ff) culminates in the third and final trill. Patches of modal ambiguity are the final hurdles in this steeplechase to definitive closure.

The ritornello that follows begins with an exhilarating burst of sound on the resolution of the third cadential trill. This "middle ritornello," in F major, consists of the only two themes from the opening ritornello that had not figured in the solo exposition: the *forte* drive to the half-cadence (*2*), now modified to cadence in the new tonic, and the *piano* closing theme (*6*). The solo exposition and the middle ritornello thus complement one another and, together, constitute a sonata-style "exposition" that may be viewed as a modified expansion of the opening ritornello, achieved through the agency of the solo. The solo contributes its own "first," "second," and "cadence" themes (N, D, and E, respectively), and it "commandeers" one ritornello to accomplish the crucial modulation to the relative major and another to bolster the arrival in that key. The middle ritornello rounds out the exposition, reinforcing the new key with cadence-directed materials. On the local level it is connected, both rhythmically and motivically, to the end of the first solo: it enters on the resolution of the cadential trill, and the downward arpeggios of its initial theme (2) are prefigured just before the trill by that same motive in the winds. On the larger structural level, the middle ritornello secures a parallel with the opening ritornello, as both end with the same theme (6).

The second solo (or "development") begins in F major with the piano playing the exposition "first theme" (N), a stereotypical choice for a sonata development, and one which carries with it the impression of beginning a second cycle or "rotation" through the sequence of exposition themes. Despite the unambiguous textural and structural break at this juncture, there is also a strong sense of continuity, particularly since the thematic sequence connecting the middle ritornello with the second solo ($6 \rightarrow N \rightarrow 1$) is the same that had earlier connected the opening ritornello with the first solo. A mirror symmetry thus orders the four main section openings, with 1 heading the outer sections (ritornello and recapitulation) and N the inner sections (exposition and development); but it is a symmetry that grows out of dramatic exigencies.[6]

The first part of the development (bars 192–229) juxtaposes these two "first" themes, which symbolize the contrasting identities of the opposed forces. The piano offers three ten-bar variants of its theme – in F major, G minor, and E-flat major – each expressing a different character and each culminating in a virtuosic cadential gesture. These alternate with four-bar passages played by the full orchestra. Restless in both mood and tonal shape, these orchestral rebuttals intrude on the solo's cadences and modulate to the key in which the next solo statement will begin. The solo thus seeks tonal stability, preferably, it would seem, in a major key, where its theme seems most at home. The orchestra, on the other hand, seems bent on undermining this aspiration and forces the harmonic journey. Its ultimate goal, of course, is the restoration of the home tonic, D minor, where it can reassert its authority by restating its theme in full. The solo meanwhile seeks to avert this inevitable capitulation – as long as possible. From that point of view, the key of E-flat major is a trap. The piano accepts it as a "safe space," realizing too late (when the orchestra fails to interrupt its cadence) that it is the key of the Neapolitan in relation to the home tonic, perilously close to that which it sought to avoid. (The Neapolitan harmony had earlier figured prominently in *5*.) Seeking escape, the piano launches in bar 230 a flurry of bravura figuration, up and down the keyboard. In a panicked response to the "crisis" it abandons its theme. To tighten its grip, the orchestra relinquishes its syncopated treble chords and assigns the bass motive to the unison strings, facilitating the forceful articulation of the underlying harmonic progression, which retraces the development's earlier sequence of tonal centers, though now consistently in minor keys: F minor, G minor, and (instead of E-flat) the dominant in D minor. This arrival, in bar 242, marks the beginning of the retransition, through which the piano continues its increasingly frantic figuration, spurred on by the winds. In bar 250 these winds drop out, leaving the piano isolated on the dominant, exhausted and trapped. In anger and frustration, it delivers the two-bar half-cadence from the middle of ritornello theme *2* (bars 21–2), turning to one of the few ritornello themes it had not already tried to claim. This buys a moment of time but does not offer a way out, leaving the solo no option but to face the inevitable and deal with the consequences. In halting steps it begins a slow chromatic ascent, twice arrested by moments of doubt, before it musters the courage to charge forward to the tonic resolution, the re-entry of the orchestra, and the start of the recapitulation.

If the recapitulation begins with the opening theme of the ritornello rather than the "new" theme of the solo exposition, it is not because this choice is normative, but because the orchestra has won that privilege. The "new" theme had dominated the first half of the development, but the solo gave it up willingly, and it will not be heard from again – unless the pianist chooses to incorporate it into the cadenza (an idea that occurred to Beethoven, and to many others before and since). Theme *1* is, in fact, common to both ritornello and exposition: in the former it was purely orchestral, while in the latter the solo intervention effected changes that forced it to a different conclusion. In the recapitulation aspects of both versions are in evidence – along with something new. The piano, stung by the experience of the development, delays its entrance until the end of the eighth bar, and its new broken-octave right-hand figuration is more overtly chromatic (and frantic) than was its contribution in the exposition. The first violins respond by relinquishing their characteristic appoggiaturas and more closely following the piano, not only in its boldly rising chromatic lines but in its two attempts, as in the exposition, to break free of the theme's original design. It succeeded in so doing in the exposition, but not here: the final two bars (bars 267–8) restore much of the ritornello reading, including the flute and oboe parts and the cadence in the tonic, though the piano's bravado seems to inspire the orchestra to abandon the syncopations of its final bar in favor of a more forthright close.

The piano has already made a difference, but not enough to redirect the recapitulation along the path of the exposition. It thus retreats momentarily, awaiting another opportunity to assert its will, as the orchestra proceeds with the next in its original sequence of ritornello themes (2). After nine bars the piano re-enters, with triplet arpeggios that overreach and overshadow the orchestral theme, enabling it, in bar 281, to introduce the exposition version of the half-cadence theme (3). From this point on, the recapitulation follows the thematic plan of the exposition, though all hope of major-key relief is dashed and the tragic outcome is foreseen when the sequence pattern of the ritornello lyric theme (4) is forced back into the minor. The distraught piano dramatizes the harmonic turning point, abandoning its façade of elegant poise for three anguished bars of angular, syncopated material (bars 296–8) that lead to a half-cadence in the home tonic, D minor. Had he wished, Mozart might easily have used the ritornello version of this theme, simply ending it in a half-cadence. Instead he has us hear this moment in relation to the exposition, forcing us to confront what has been lost and the cost associated with that loss.

The solo "second theme" (D) is now in D minor. Formerly an expression of hope, it now speaks of resignation and despair. The transformation of major-key themes into the minor is a specialty of Mozart's, and how he accomplishes it is always wonderful and unpredictable. Here the telling twist is the use of the Neapolitan sixth chord, the harmony that marked the turning point in the development and will have further significance as the movement unfolds. The beginning of the solo "coda" (*E*) is also transformed beyond the switch in modality. Heavy-hearted, its formerly optimistic rising contours are literally downcast. The coda again unfolds in three stages, culminating in trills, but each is now prolonged. Instead of 10+6+15 (=31) bars, the proportions are 12+8+18 (=38). Adding to the increased excitement is the greater presence of the orchestra, especially the off-beat wind chords, building to the dramatic arrival on the Neapolitan sixth in bar 348.

The ritornello to the cadenza, like the middle ritornello, begins with the "*forte* drive to the dominant" (*2*), but once it reaches its central half-cadence – the same cadence that marked the solo's point of terminal frustration at the end of the development – a series of chords progresses to the cadential six-four for the solo cadenza. Following the cadenza, the ritornello resumes with the closing themes of the opening ritornello (*5* and *6*), though the former is streamlined through the suppression of internal repetitions. It has no need for extraneous display, the game having been decisively won. In its two previous appearances, at the ends of the opening and middle ritornellos, theme *6* had provided closure and was succeeded by *N*, in the same key. It is followed now neither by that theme nor by a celebratory flourish, but by a new variant of the opening syncopated theme (*1*), the theme which, by rights, might have begun the exposition and development had it not been for the intervention of the solo. By this point in the movement – and regardless of the cadenza – the solo theme and the aspirations it represented have been effectively annihilated. There could be no better way to symbolize this tragic outcome than by breaking the very "cycle" of thematic order that had led to its appearances and, moreover, by replacing it with its nemesis. Hushed and somewhat subdued, the opening theme now finds some measure of repose through its new subdominant emphasis, as its syncopations give way to a series of calm closing cadences. Still accompanied by the unsettling bass figure (though that now sounds more like a distant funeral march), it fades away into the only *pianissimo* of the entire movement, while high above, the flute (bars 394–5) offers a knowing reminder of and rejoinder to the piano's futile stirring at the end of the development. On a purely formal level, this tonic resolution of the former half-cadence figure creates symmetrical closure in relation to the end of the development, effectively tying up a loose end. The storm may have subsided, but as we will discover in the next two movements, it remains an ominous threat.

For a movement that is so passionate and impulsive, it is at first surprising to discover that it is so highly ordered and regular in form. This concerto has often been called Beethovenian, an association the later composer himself encouraged when he supplied it with cadenzas – cadenzas that have remained, and are likely to remain, unsurpassed. The most obvious connection is in the often tempestuous nature of the materials themselves, coupled with a motivic homogeneity that promotes a sense that the music is self-generating and therefore seems predestined. The structural regularity and logic that govern the organization of these materials leave no room for whim, and promote thereby a feeling of inevitability and white-hot intensity. At least, this must have been how Beethoven heard it.

K. 467: Allegro maestoso[7]

The opening theme of K. 467 reverts to the march-like character of the concertos of 1784, but with an important difference. In contrast to their homophonic settings, this march begins with unison strings, suggesting developmental and even contrapuntal possibilities that are indeed to be its destiny. A contrapuntally suggestive unison opening is not without precedent. One has only to go back to the Piano Concerto in E-flat, K. 449, completed in February 1784 but probably begun in 1782, though perhaps an even more striking antecedent may be found in the Piano Concerto in C, K. 415/387b, of 1782–3, which opens with a three-part canon in the strings, presenting a subject whose motives reappear in some subsequent themes. But in neither of these earlier works do we find the contrapuntal potential of the opening so fully realized on the larger structural level as it is in K. 467, where various polyphonic settings of the opening theme produce some of the main structural blocks of the ritornello. This makes for a homogeneity and continuity even more compelling than that of K. 466, achieved through rather different means and with materials that are obviously in a completely different character.

Charles Rosen has described K. 467 as "Mozart's first true essay in orchestral grandeur" and has commented on the block-like nature of its construction, evident not only in the laying out of themes but in their

43

scoring, which often juxtaposes "masses" of sounds.[8] The winds, for example, are more likely to be deployed as a section than as individual voices, as in their initial appearances, when, together with trumpets and timpani, they assemble as a corps to answer the strings with wind-band fanfares epitomizing the march *topos* that has been implicit from the beginning. In keeping with the march character, the harmonization of this *piano* opening theme (Fig. 2: *1*) is strictly limited to tonic and dominant chords. Bar 12 brings the "*forte* move to the dominant" (Fig. 2: *2*). As in K. 466, this dynamic shift marks the first time the entire orchestra plays together, intensity is maintained by string tremolos, and the material presented is a transformed restatement of the opening theme. The nature of that transformation is, of course, quite different though not unrelated. If in K. 466 the bass figure gained prominence and a new character by moving up into the violins, in K. 467 the four-bar unison theme is consigned to the bass while a countermelody of sorts is added above it. This passage culminates in a lengthy dominant pedal, supporting a rising melodic sequence based on the fourth bar of the opening theme (Fig. 2: *3*).

Rather than allow a pause to follow the half-cadence, as he had done so dramatically in K. 466, Mozart fills in the two-bar caesura with light-hearted descending scales, marked *piano*, which transform the character of the music while sustaining its continuity. The so-called "lyric" theme (Fig. 2: *4A*) is then announced by a triadic "horn-call" figure. Sounded by the horns and trumpets and supported by a *Trommelbass* in the lower strings, the horn-call initiates a dialogue between brass and winds that restores some of the movement's original martial flavor. The march *topos* having been recovered, the opening theme returns as well, succeeding the cadence of the "lyric" theme with imitative presentations of the opening two-bar motto (Fig. 2: *4B*). The two-bar ostinato that results from the regular overlap of the tonic and dominant forms of this motto produces considerable momentum as it unfolds over a dominant pedal. The dynamic level meanwhile increases to *forte* as more and more instruments enter, until the entire orchestra is reassembled. The "regular" closing themes (Fig. 2: *5, 6,* and *7*) then follow, arranged in the stereotypical *forte–piano–forte* pattern. The last of these is a "flourish" based, once again, on the opening motto, which is presented in quasi-imitative fashion. Its triadic makeup, rhythmic regimentation, and harmonic

Figure 2 *K. 467/I, organization*

RITORNELLO

R1 (67 bars)

bar	1	12	20	28	36	44	52	64	68	74
theme	**1**	**2**	**3**	**4A**	**4B**	**5**	**6**	**7**		solo entrance
key	C									V/C-------

(12 bars)

EXPOSITION

S1 (114 bars)   **R2** (28 bars)

bar	80	91	107	109	122	128	143	148	169	194	205
theme	*1*	*A*	*B*	*C*	*BB*	*D*	*4B*	*E1*	*E2*	**2**	**6**
key	C	V/C	g		V/g–V/G	G			G		V/e

DEVELOPMENT

S2 (52 bars)

bar	222	237	241	245	249	259	266	270
theme	*N*	*(E2)*	*(E2)*	*(E2)*	*(E2)*	*(6)*	*(E1)*	*(E1)*
key	e	V/a	V/d	V/g	V/c	(c)	V/c	V/C

RECAPITULATION

R3 (23 bars)   **S3** (87 bars)   **R4** (13+21 = 34 bars)

bar	274	285	295	297	301	305	313	328	333	347	351	359	384	397	405	409	413
theme	*1*	*2*	*4B/4B*	*C'*	*BB*	*D*	*4B*	*E1*	*3'*	*4A*	*E2*	*2*	*2*	**5**	**6**	**7**	**8**
key	C	F	f	V/c–V/C	C						cadenza						

≈R1   !   ≈S1   ≈R1   ≈S1 ≈R2   ≈R1

= NEW

Themes *2*, *3*, *4B*, **7**, **8**, and *E1* are all based on Theme 1 or its motives. Tutti themes are shown in boldface.

simplicity come as a sharp rebuke to the chromaticism and the destabilizing, minor-inflected harmonies that color the previous closing themes.

The motivic unity of the opening ritornello is striking. While the schema of differentiated functional units adheres closely to the generic model, the bulk of the ritornello – themes *1*, *2*, *3*, *4B*, and *7* – is explicitly derived from the opening motto. This thematic unity is matched by a striking rhythmic regularity. As Rosen has observed, four-bar phrases predominate, contributing to a remarkable "rhythmic breadth."

Is the piano intimidated by the orchestra's show of force and, like Cherubino, reluctant to don military garb? Whatever the reason, rather than bow out and relinquish the stage, as is the norm, the orchestra drops to a less intimidating dynamic level and dispatches a succession of woodwind emissaries to cajole the soloist into entering. Each of these invitations ends on an expectant dominant, preceded by increasingly urgent pre-dominant harmonies.[9] The third time's the charm, as the piano enters on the dominant with flurries of sixteenth-note passagework. More athletic and acrobatic than combative, it begins in spurts, initially egged on by urgently repeating, exhortative string chords. Once launched, it soars, rising to the highest note of the fortepiano keyboard, the seventh of the dominant seventh chord and the point of departure for an *Eingang*, which must be inserted to provide a link to the beginning of the solo exposition. In the autograph score Mozart left space for this *Eingang* – a full page, in fact – but, regrettably, he never filled it in. This blank page remains a tantalizing reminder of our loss.[10]

This virtuosic solo entrance (with the nature and degree of virtuosity established by Mozart in bars 74–8, but limited only by the player's own inclinations and imagination in the "improvised" *Eingang* at bar 79) establishes the solo presence so forcefully that its stature is undiminished when it steps back and sustains a long held trill while the orchestral strings launch the exposition proper with their unison opening theme (*1*). In the theme's fifth bar (bar 84) the piano takes over, unaccompanied. A gymnast rather than a fighter, the solo replaces the dotted rhythms of the martial wind-band fanfares with graceful turns and chromatic passing tones, and indulges in lively decorative figuration when the orchestra re-enters at bar 88 for the balance of the theme. The exposition version of theme *1* is thus a marvelous blend of the old and new, with the solo assuming leadership by personalizing the material and perpetuating a virtuoso presence. The eventual restoration of the jaunty wind fanfare (bar 90) has some of the effect of the orchestra's "cadential flourish on the tonic" (7), an option at this point in the Leeson–Levin model, though here the flourish is built into the theme itself.

At this point, the solo takes the lead in moving the exposition through themes that are mostly new, even if important motivic connections can be identified. The *sujet libre* (Fig. 2: *A*) begins with the piano alone. After an opening theme harmonized with nothing but tonic and dominant chords, Mozart's telling use of the subdominant and the expressive appoggiaturas bring warmth to the solo utterance – to a degree previously lacking in the movement. But with the return of the strings, the solo becomes more animated and drives toward a half-cadence on the dominant. This harmonic arrival is prolonged for two bars by the full orchestra, entering *forte* (Fig. 2: *B*). Using a forceful rising anacrusis figure, it ascends two octaves, decorating a G-major arpeggio. The solo, clearly inspired by this arpeggio, re-enters with a bold triadic theme, treating this dominant chord as a tonic, but with a surprising modal shift into G minor. This minor-key "detour" delays the arrival of the "second theme" and thus represents the "episode" that introduces, but does not yet assert, the dominant tonality (Fig. 2: *C*). This highly expressive G-minor melody, whose poignant appoggiaturas seem to anticipate the G-minor Symphony, K. 550, "thematizes" the modulation and identifies the soloist as the modulatory agent as it moves toward a half-cadence *in* the dominant. The Leeson–Levin model calls for the orchestra to articulate this half-cadence, and the strings do return at this point (Fig. 2: *BB*, at bar 122), but the piano continues to dominate, with chromatic passagework. Moreover, the strings support the wrong tonality (V of G *minor*), requiring the unaccompanied piano to make the modal correction and provide the link to the "second theme."

For its "second theme" the solo, which has long been directing and dominating the proceedings, declines to adopt the ritornello's "horn-call" (*4A*) and instead introduces a sunny new theme in G major (Fig. 2: *D*). This independent streak comes to an end when, following the theme's concluding cadence, the piano surprisingly reverts to ritornello material – *4B*, the imitative version of the opening motto – to begin the "coda." The orchestral instruments, unable to resist the appeal of imitative play, follow suit and take over the motto, thus freeing the soloist to warm up, with limbering tremolos and arpeggio pirouettes, for the dazzling acrobatics that follow (Fig. 2: *E*). Theme *4B* therefore serves the same function in the exposition that it had in the ritornello – of following the "second" theme and initiating the closing themes.

The balance of the "coda" (*E*) is quite extended. It contains a variety of materials and unfolds in three spans, each ending in a cadential trill. A somewhat detailed description is necessary to prepare the listener for the ways in which Mozart varies and rearranges these materials in the recapitulation (see Figure 3). The "coda" flows directly out of *4B*, reaching a four-bar sequential "block" in bars 154–7, material that forms the core of each of the three approaches to cadential closure. In the first of these spans the "block" ends in a half-cadence (bars 158–60) with a motive related to bars 24–5 of *3*, the ritornello half-cadence theme. (The presence of this material will have significant ramifications for the recapitulation.) A more lyrical continuation of this passage leads to the first cadential trill, the stereotypical signal of closure, but this trill is too short and in too low a register to be truly conclusive. The solo thus resumes its exuberant gymnastics for a second bid, offering in bars 171–4 a varied restatement of the four-bar "block" and closing with the second cadential trill, in the "proper" high register but still too short. For the third and final segment of the "coda," the piano uses the stock variation technique of having right and left hands switch parts to vary the previous eight-bar segment (bars 178–85 corresponding to bars 169–76, encompassing the four-bar "block" plus two bars on either side). Excitement mounts as the strings and winds join in, and the piano concludes the solo exposition with the third trill, finally a full bar long and in the proper high register. As in the analogous section of K. 466, Mozart twice teases the listener with the promise of closure before the actual conclusion.

The middle ritornello begins *forte* with the the full orchestra and consists of only two themes drawn from the opening ritornello – *2* and *6* – just as in K. 466. Since theme *2* is based on the opening motive (as it was in K. 466), it suggests a section beginning, while at the same time its ending is altered to cadence in the dominant key, thus reinforcing the tonal goal of the solo exposition. Mozart effected this change via the dominant's flat submediant (E-flat). The arresting jagged bass line at this point (bars 199–204), a repeated oscillation between *d* and *e♭*, has

Figure 3 *K. 467/1, plan of Theme* E, *exposition and recapitulation*

PLAN OF THEME *E* (exposition):

E1

bars	148–53	154–7	158–60	161–8
theme	*(4B)*	BLOCK	*(3')*	ends in trill

E2

	169–70 / 171–4 / 175–6	177
	BLOCK	ends in trill
	178–9 / 180–3 / 184–5	186–93
	BLOCK	ends in trill

PLAN OF THEME *E* (recapitulation):

E1

bars	333–8	339–42	343–6	*3'* 347–50	*4A* 351–8
theme	*(4B)*	BLOCK	*(3')*	end of *3*	*4A*

E2

	359–62 / 363	364–5
	BLOCK	ends in trill
	366–9 / 370	371–83
	BLOCK	ends in trill

51

motivic significance, having been heard repeatedly and prominently at key points in the solo exposition: in the G-minor episode (*C*, bars 110–14), the "second theme" (*D*, bars 140–1), and the "coda" (*E*, bars 158–9). The *piano* closing theme which follows (*6*) is also modified, but in the opposite direction. Instead of cadencing in G major, it modulates to E minor and concludes the ritornello on an expectant dominant chord in that key. The tonal shift is symbolized by the handling of the note *e♭*, which, as the bass of an augmented-sixth chord, resolves to *d* in bars 203–4 and 213–14 but is enharmonically re-spelled as *d♯* and resolves to *e* in bars 206–7, 210–11, 212–13, and repeatedly throughout 215–20. (The seeds for the juxtaposition of these two enharmonic spellings – *d♯* and *e♭* – were planted early: in the initial presentation of theme *2*, bars 17–19.)

The piano plays continually throughout the perpetual-motion development (S2). It begins poignantly in E minor, accompanied by the violins, with what is ostensibly a "new" theme (Fig. 2:*N*), though its second bar (bar 223) is clearly derived from bar 2 of the opening march. In character and shape it also uncannily recalls the solo entrance of K. 466, down to the accompanying violins, which reproduce the piano left hand in the earlier concerto (compare Examples 2a and b). This connection is of more than incidental significance, since the development of K. 467, mired in minor keys and full of yearning, disquiet, and foreboding, appears to be invaded by the spirit of K. 466. The "new" development theme of K. 467 takes the form of a regular eight-bar phrase, which is then varied by the winds – flute and oboe "simplify" the theme into a starker, more plaintive utterance, which is imitated by the bassoons (Example 2c) – while the strings provide harmonic support and the piano paces uneasily. The wind abstraction of the development theme points up another relationship – to the "horn-call" of *4A* (bar 28), showing that even this most jubilant of themes has the potential for sorrow. At bar 237 the theme's expected E-minor close is interrupted and the mood is shattered, as the piano, no longer able to contain itself, begins a searching sequence through the dominants of a chain of minor keys, its agitated passagework based on bars 169–70 from the second span of *E*, but lacking the confidence it had then. When C minor is reached, a long chromatic ascent rises to a point of extreme tension on a high *e♭*, followed by the retransition over a dominant pedal. The piano's arpeggios at this point recall the pirouettes that had launched the "coda"

Example 2a K. 467/I

Example 2b K. 466/I

Example 2c K. 467/I

(bar 147), and they peak alternately on *d* and *e♭*, invoking the oscillating motive that has regularly represented modal ambivalence. That ambivalence is now resolved in favor of the major (the home tonic, C major) through a descending diatonic scale, which counters the earlier chromatic ascent and, for the first time in the development, inspires the participation of the full orchestra. The recapitulation is thus prepared, both tonally and orchestrationally.

The recapitulation begins with a substantial tutti section (R3): twenty-three bars in length, it is far longer than in any other Mozart concerto. The orchestra presents the ritornello versions of themes *1* and *2*, but not without telling changes. The former is enriched, in bars 282–3, by the horns' superimposition (with trumpet and timpani support) of the jubilant "horn-call" figure from *4A*, thus offsetting, at the earliest possible opportunity, the horn-call's minor-key transformation in the

53

development while simultaneously offering a premonition of things to come. And theme *2*, rather than ending on a dominant chord, as it had in the ritornello, or on a tonic chord (in the dominant key), as it had in the second tutti, is extended to end on the threshold of the subdominant (F major), in which key it introduces *4B*, the imitative version of the opening motto. Mozart often uses the subdominant key after (or, rarely, at) the point of recapitulation to stabilize the tonic, and to fulfill this harmonic function he skips ahead to theme *4B*, bypassing – but only for the moment – themes *3* and *4A*.

As its label implies, *4B* is, in Leeson–Levin terms, an "extraneous" theme that originally followed *4A*, the "lyric" theme of the ritornello, to rebuild momentum for the closing themes. In the exposition it analogously attached itself to *D*, the "second" theme, where it was used by the soloist to lure in the orchestra for the beginning of the "coda." Turnabout is fair play, as the orchestra now uses the theme to coax the soloist to re-enter. The theme's surprising appearance early in the recapitulation may thus be viewed as an exploitation and celebration of its superfluity: It appears prematurely and out of order, performing a new harmonic function specific to the recapitulation and serving as the unexpected vehicle for the solo re-entrance. Although it comes as a surprise, there is logic to Mozart's selection of this theme for this purpose (Tovey's "unexpected and inevitable"). Aside from theme *1*, *4B* is the only theme common to both ritornello and solo exposition, so it makes sense that it be used as a structural pivot, marking the point at which the recapitulation stops following ritornello themes and, through the presence and actions of the piano, begins to follow exposition themes. The solo entrance (and thus the beginning of S3) seems not only surprising but almost nonchalant since it occurs in mid-theme. However, after only two bars the solo imposes a somber tone as it directs the music into F minor. In that key it introduces a theme (Fig. 2: C^I, bar 301) whose shape and accompaniment may recall *D*, but whose modality and "harmonic structure," as Charles Rosen observed, are derived from *C*, the solo's minor-key episode in the exposition. The latter relationship is confirmed by the correspondence of bar 304 with bar 121 (the last bar of *C* in the exposition) and by the fact that, like theme *C* in the exposition, C^I proceeds to the half-cadence *BB*. This half-cadence is first in C *minor* (signaled in bars 305–7 by the alternation of *d* and *e*♭ in the second violins of the accompanying strings). But as soon as the strings drop out, the solo passagework "corrects" the modality and sustains the dominant of C *major* for six bars, the final four of which are supported by refreshing wind chords. (This orchestrational touch was lacking in the exposition.)

Having taken command of both thematic order and tonal direction, the solo continues with its "second" theme (*D*), after which *4B* returns in its "proper" position. As in the exposition, the "coda" theme (*E*) then follows, though initially with greater polyphonic density: while the strings exchange statements of the *first* bar of the march motto, the bassoons now trade sequential statements of its *second* bar (bars 333–8; see Fig. 3). At bar 347, however, the departure from the exposition model is even more radical, when the brief allusion to *3* (*3'*, in bars 343–6) blossoms into a more extended quotation of that theme, which has not been heard since the opening ritornello, more than 300 bars earlier (compare bars 347–50 with bars 24–7). This reference opens the way for the orchestra to regain control of the recapitulation with its "horn-call" theme, *4A*. The two themes that invade the solo "coda," *3* and *4A*, are the very ones that had been "skipped" in the recapitulatory tutti (R2). The scoring of *4A* is here reinforced to ring out with greater force and thus celebrate its belated restoration after having been long suppressed and, in the development, rendered dispirited through its transformed incorporation into the plaintive version of theme *N* (winds, bars 231–4). The piano joins in the festivities by re-entering for the consequent phrase. The "skipped" themes having been recovered (and there being no need for yet another statement of *4B*), the piano resumes the "coda," but without the bars that had contributed to the agitated sequences of the development. Mozart's suave rewriting of the piano right hand in bars 359–61 (in comparison with bars 171–3) shows the composer forced to conform to the upper limit of his keyboard (*f'''*) but doing so in a manner that turns the limitation to his advantage.

Parallel to the middle ritornello, the ritornello leading to the cadenza also uses theme *2*, and in the same modified form (emphasizing the submediant), though it culminates here in a cadential six-four chord to usher in the cadenza. The ritornello following the cadenza mirrors the end of the opening ritornello and its three closing themes. The two *forte* themes (*5* and *7*), which have not been heard since the opening ritornello, are given in full, but the intervening *piano* theme (*6*), which had appeared in the middle ritornello, is limited to its first four bars, with the resulting suppression of its patch of modal ambiguity. To this succession of closing themes Mozart adds a fourth, the concluding flourish (*8*, bars 413–17). The flourish begins with the winds definitively settling the $e\flat$–$d\sharp$ question in favor of the latter by playfully and repeatedly resolving the $d\sharp$ to e, supported by a C-major chord (bars 413–14). Meanwhile the strings and brass twice ascend through the notes of the C-major triad, as if "correcting" the modality of the minor-key theme *C*, whose opening is here recalled. Finally, in bars 415–16, the strings present a whimsical new form of the opening motto, giving the impression that its two bars are being presented in reverse order[11] – a concise and witty symbol of the large-scale structural reordering that has marked the recapitulation.

Tovey observed that concerto recapitulations were of both the opening tutti and the first solo, and this principle is quite apparent here. The recapitulation in K. 467 is far less regular or predictable than that of K. 466, and that unpredictability is in keeping with its high-spirited character. Nevertheless, all of the themes from the opening ritornello return in the recapitulation, if not in their entirety or in their original order. The first solo, on the other hand, is not as completely represented: themes *A*, *B*, and much of *C* are lacking, as are parts of *E*. Mozart's cadenza for this movement has not survived, but pianists wishing to write or improvise their own might consider including these "neglected" themes.

4

Middle movements

K. 466: Romance

While all of Mozart's concerto first movements share the same basic formal scheme, his middle movements display a variety of forms and types. To make matters even more complicated, they have been described and categorized by different commentators using a sometimes bewildering assortment of nomenclature and terminology.[1] In order to avoid having to define distinctions, on the one hand, among possible meanings of "concerto" form, "quasi-concerto" form, "concertino" form, "sonata" form, "sonatina" form, and "binary" form, and, on the other hand, between "ternary" form and "da capo aria" form, we may simplify the taxonomy of piano-concerto second movements by dividing them into four basic formal categories: (1) "first-movement" form (with a full or abbreviated opening "ritornello" or introduction; with subsequent ritornellos present, vestigial, or nonexistent; and with or without "development"), (2) ternary form, (3) rondo form, and (4) variation form. In terms of tonality, relative to the key of the outer movements, the middle movements may be in the subdominant, the submediant, the dominant, or, in the case of the C-minor Concerto, K. 491, the mediant (relative major).[2]

The second movement of the D-minor Concerto is in the submediant, B-flat major. It lacks a tempo marking but is in alla breve and is titled "Romance," a heading that it shares with five other instrumental slow movements by Mozart: in the Serenade ["Gran Partitta"] in B-flat, K. 361/370a (marked "Adagio–Allegretto–Adagio"), probably of 1781–2; the Divertimento in B-flat, K. Anh. 229/439b No. 5, for three basset horns ("Andante"), from ?1783 or later; the Horn Concerto in E-flat, K. 495 ("Andante cantabile"), of 1786; and the Horn Concerto in E-flat, K. 447 ("Larghetto"), and the string serenade *Eine kleine Nacht-musik*, K. 525 ("Andante"), both of 1787.[3]

In early-eighteenth-century France, the *romance* was a strophic lyric poem which typically recounted a sentimental love story set in ancient times. Musical settings of the *romance* – in strophic form, with simple melodies and subsidiary accompaniments – were popular in the mid-century *opéra comique*. Jean-Jacques Rousseau, an early exponent of the genre, prescribed the appropriate musical style in his *Dictionnaire de musique* (1768), which defined the musical setting of the *romance* as an

> Air to which is sung a little poem of the same name, divided into verse [couplets], of which the subject is ordinarily some amorous tale, and often tragic. As the romance should be simple, touching, and somewhat archaic in style, the air should correspond to the character of the words: no orna-ments, nothing mannered, the melody gentle, natural, rustic and pro-ducing its effect by itself, independently of the manner in which it is sung. The melody need not be piquant; it suffices that it be naïve, that it does not go against the words, that it makes them easily intelligible, and that it does not demand an extended vocal compass. A well-written romance, having no salient features, makes no impression at first, but each verse [couplet] adds something to the effect of the preceding verses, augmenting the interest imperceptibly, and sometimes one finds oneself moved to tears without being able to say wherein lies the charm that brought this about. It is a common experience that all instrumental accompaniment weakens this impression. The only thing needed for the melody of the romance is a voice that is in tune, clear, articulating the words well and singing simply.[4]

Early musical settings of the *romance* were strophic, but later examples sometimes alternated sections in major and minor keys or introduced strophic variation.[5] The German *Romanze* was evidently influenced by the French example (see, for example, Pedrillo's narrative *Romanze* "In Mohrenland gefangen war" in Mozart's 1782 *Singspiel Die Entführung aus dem Serail*), and in both countries the style of the *romance* was trans-ferred to instrumental compositions. The instrumental *romance*, typ-ically in ternary, rondo, or variation form, could serve as the slow movement of a symphony, concerto, serenade, or string quartet. The French composer François-Joseph Gossec was apparently the first to have used it in a symphony (in Paris, around 1761–2), while Carl Ditters von Dittersdorf is believed to have introduced it to Vienna in 1773.[6] One of Haydn's "Paris" Symphonies, No. 85 ("La reine"), of 1785 or 1786 (and thus roughly contemporary with K. 466), includes a variation-form *Romanze* based on the French song "La gentille et jeune Lisette."

Heinrich Christoph Koch, in his *Introductory Essay on Composition* (*Versuch einer Anleitung zur Composition*, 1782–93), commented on the increasing use of the *romance* as the slow movement of a concerto: "In the more modern concertos, . . . instead of the customary adagio, often a so-called romance is composed. This has a definite character, which one can best get to know from Sulzer's description [in his *Allgemeine Theorie*] of the romance in poetry. 'Nowadays,' says Sulzer, 'the name romance is given to short narrative songs in the extremely simple and antiquated tone of the old rhymed romances. Their content may be a passionate, tragic, amorous, or even merely entertaining narrative. ["In music," interjects Koch in a footnote, "this last type of romance is not used, because now it is composed only in slow tempo."] . . . Ideas and expression must be of the utmost simplicity and very naive.' "[7]

By virtue of its tempo, the "slow" movement of any concerto is bound to offer contrast, and in minor-key concertos the characteristic use of a major key for this movement contributes moreover a feeling of relief. In the case of K. 466, however, the *romance* promises not just relief from the tragic mood of the opening movement, but a sense of escape as well, made immediately apparent when the piano opens the movement unaccompanied and without benefit – or constraint – of an introductory orchestral ritornello, as if having broken free of the terms and agenda previously imposed by the orchestra. Since the piano melody is self-accompanied, it does not exactly comply with Rousseau's suggestion that the vocal *romance* be unaccompanied (nor, for that matter, did Rousseau's own *romances*[8]), but its essential *romance* character – simple, gentle, naive, natural – is decidedly enhanced by the absence of the orchestra. This is the very first of Mozart's piano-concerto slow movements to begin with the solo, but it set the pattern for four of his seven remaining works in the genre, K. 488, K. 491, K. 537, and K. 595, all of which are in ternary or rondo form, and the last three of which are *romance*-like in character, even if they are not so titled.[9] (Similarly, the slow movements of Mozart's last three wind concertos – the two Horn Concerto Romances and the Adagio of the Clarinet Concerto, K. 622 – open with the solo, though accompanied by the strings.) In K. 466,

Mozart's precedent-setting decision to begin the Romance with an unaccompanied solo was not his original conception, but it was apparently an almost instantaneous second thought: in the autograph he initially indicated a dynamic marking (*piano*) for the first violins, but he crossed it out before writing a note of music in their part.[10]

The deliberate naiveté of the K. 466 Romance is easily misunderstood. Arthur Hutchings, for example, described the opening theme as "graceful and limpid, but . . . not particularly inspired." He went on to editorialize: "Mozart at his most pedestrian, like Pope, was such a master of the craft of his age that his stock-in-trade becomes enjoyable to audiences with whom it has the charm of a fragrant past."[11] In this last observation, however, he unwittingly stumbled onto one of the music's essential features, which it derives from the poetic *romance* – that, in the words of Rousseau, it be "somewhat archaic in style." This evocation of a past, and of a lost innocence, certainly contributes to the poignancy of the music, and presumably this quality would have been sensed even by Mozart's audience. It may be going too far to hear in the pedal-point "drone" and gentle rocking motion of the opening phrase a hint of the rustic or the pastoral, but these features add to the subtle sense of longing or even nostalgia that lies beneath the music's surface simplicity. (It is also possible to link the half-step rocking motivically and hermeneutically to the very end of the preceding movement, particularly the oscillating flute line, which shares the same alternating pitches – *d* and *c*♯ – with the piano's middle voice.)

According to Koch, the concerto *romance* was usually a rondo, and that is the case in K. 466, where the essential form may be diagrammed as *ABACA*. The main, recurring melody (*A*; see Example 3) adheres to a "lyric form" common to the vocal *romance* (*aa′ba′*), and its underlying binary structure is articulated by a repetition scheme that alternates solo and orchestral statements of the phrase pairs: ‖: *aa′* :‖‖: *ba′* :‖. The orchestral renditions introduce minor decorative variants to the melody and, in contrast to the dynamically uniform piano statements, impose a more overtly expressive dynamic scheme that systematically divides each of the four phrases into two bars of *forte* (winds and strings) followed by two bars of *piano* (mostly strings only). This pattern of loud–soft dynamic retreat has the effect of constantly pulling back or drawing inward. This tendency toward introversion or introspection is reversed, however, in

Example 3 K. 466/II, themes

the extension that the orchestra appends to the end of the melody, which blossoms through a long *crescendo* into a *forte* close. But this, too, is followed by a quiet four-bar cadential tag, a codetta that brings the opening section to a close with a graceful bow.

The *B* theme (at bar 40; see Example 3) is presented entirely by the piano with discreet string accompaniment and is somewhat more operatic and extroverted. It reflects *romance* simplicity and naiveté by continuing the prevailing pattern of regular four-bar phrases, but it is more varied rhythmically and moves by leaps into a higher tessitura. Beginning in the tonic (and over a tonic pedal), it passes through the dominant minor (a hint of things to come) on its way to the dominant major, F major. There it closes, adding the same graceful cadential tag that had concluded the *A* section. On the final cadence, however, the winds enter to guide the solo's short retransition to the tonic key for the return of the opening theme (bar 68), of which only the first half (*aa′*) is offered, played first by the solo and then by the orchestra.

A minor-key episode is a common feature of Mozart's instrumental *romances*, and it may reflect a similar option in the vocal *romance*. We find it in the Horn Concerto, K. 495, in *Eine kleine Nachtmusik*, and in the Serenade, K. 361/370a, where the contrast is not merely in tonality (C minor vs. E-flat major), but also in tempo (Allegretto vs. Adagio) and in meter (2/4 vs. 3/4). In K. 466 the contrast is equally arresting, and

61

Charles Rosen has astutely commented that such an "eruption of violence" is explicable only in the context of the work as a whole, with its minor-key outer movements.[12] It is perhaps the return of the storm that had subsided at the end of the opening Allegro. The dramatic *C* episode (at bar 84; see Example 3) begins abruptly in G minor with a striking change in texture: an agitated, almost breathless solo part marked by hand-crossing and continuous rapid triplet figuration, countermelodies in the winds, and isolated *forte* hammer blows in the strings. There is a natural temptation to speed up at this point, although Leopold Mozart implied, in a letter of 4 January 1786 to his daughter, that a single tempo should be maintained throughout the movement. He wrote: "[In the] Romance, the tempo is to be taken at the speed in which the noisy passage with the fast triplets . . . can be executed, and these must be properly practiced so that the theme is not too lifeless. In the same way the tempo of the first Allegro must be taken according to the fast passages."[13] Leopold's admonition, however, indicates a concern that Nannerl might not play the "noisy" section fast enough, whereas when modern pianists introduce a change of tempo it is more likely because they have played the opening of the movement too slowly.

Like the refrain, the *C* episode is a self-contained lyric form: $\|: x :\|: y\ x' :\|$. Its energy spills over into a codetta and retransition, in the course of which calm is eventually restored (along with the original B-flat tonality). The *A* refrain now returns in full (bar 119), except that the orchestral repeat of the opening strain is omitted. This allows the piano to present the entire melody as an unaccompanied solo, its touching simplicity providing maximal contrast with the preceding storm. When the orchestra enters for the repeat of the second strain, it appends the extension of its opening statement, though the piano now joins in, tracing delicate arpeggios up and down the keyboard. The coda (bar 146), introduced by the winds, recalls the *B* episode and, with its subdominant emphasis, promises a peaceful close. The movement ends with a nostalgic looking back – to the same graceful codetta that had concluded the first *A* and *B* sections.

A problem for the soloist is how to deal with the many repetitions of the opening phrase. In the course of the movement it appears fourteen times, eight of them played by the piano. Progressively more elaborate improvised embellishment would be an obvious solution, but it might be misguided. As Daniel Gottlob Türk wrote in his *School of Clavier Playing* (*Klavierschule*) of 1789: "The *Romanze*, which is now making its way into instrumental music, must have a simple, agreeable, and naïve melody appropriate to its original purpose, as has already been quite correctly remarked by Rousseau. The player must carefully guard against ornaments and additions above all, for the simple melody will be ennobled and made more poignant by increasing expression rather than by ornaments and additions."[14]

K. 467: Andante

Thanks to the 1967 Swedish film *Elvira Madigan* the Andante of K. 467 is today probably the most popular and best known of Mozart's concerto movements. This middle-brow "art" film (Ingmar Bergman for the masses) had great appeal at the time of its release, though it is largely forgotten today (one must hunt in a well-stocked video store to find it). Set in 1889, the film portrays the doomed romance of an AWOL Swedish army lieutenant and a Danish tightrope dancer. As a popular film guide notes, its "attractive stars, lovers-on-the-run theme, and lovely soft-focus photography made this click with [the] public," although it was "stylistically a bit too much like a shampoo commercial."[15] Throughout the movie, fragments of the Andante from K. 467 (mostly drawn from the opening ritornello) accompany the lovers' idyllic private moments of shared affection. Thirty years after the film's release its association with Mozart's music persists. Even Deutsche Grammophon's recent series of CD reissues, called "The Originals," sought to capitalize on the connection when it "packaged" Geza Anda's performance of K. 467 not with a reproduction of the "original" LP cover from 1962, but with that of the LP reissue: a still from the movie depicting the title character and the legend "The original performance featured in *Elvira Madigan*."

Critics disagree as to the form of the Andante. Girdlestone offers a diagram that divides it into three periods (pp. 342–3) but states elsewhere that it does "not correspond to any fixed plan" (p. 47). Hutchings invents a category, "irregular non-strophic" (p. 17), that describes not what it is, but what it is not; he later calls it binary (p. 140). To Charles Rosen, it looks like a sonata but has characteristics of rondo form and sounds like an improvisation (*Classical Style*, pp. 238–9). Tischler calls it

Figure 4 *K. 414/385p, organization of Andante (tutti themes in boldface)*

	RIT.		EXPO.				DEV.	RECAP.			
	R1		***S1***				***R2***	***S2***		***R3***	***R4***
theme	*1 4 5 6*		*1 C 4 E*				*5 6*	*"6"*	*1 4 E "E"*	cadenza	*5 6*
key	I		I V V				V	v → I	I		I

"concerto form" (i.e., first-movement form), as does James Webster, who adds the qualifier "rounded binary" to reflect the non-tonic beginning of the recapitulation.[16]

As Carl Schachter suggests through the title of his article, "Idiosyncratic Features of Three Mozart Slow Movements: The Piano Concertos K. 449, K. 453, and K. 467," much of the taxonomic confusion stems from structural peculiarities unique to the movement.[17] However, some of the difficulty arises from basic differences between first- and second-movement concerto form. To explore these differences, the Andante of K. 467 may profitably be considered in relation to two other concerto-form Andantes, one earlier (in A major, K. 414/385p, of 1782) and one later (in C major, K. 503, of 1786). To facilitate comparison with first-movement form, the Leeson–Levin labeling system will be employed. It goes without saying that the slower tempi of the middle movements means that, in comparison with Allegros, they must have fewer and "shorter" themes (as measured by bars). Therefore, certain structural elements of first-movement form will of necessity be omitted. As a corollary, dynamics will generally play a smaller role in differentiating thematic units.

A diagram of the Andante of K. 414/385p illustrates its close resemblance to first-movement form (see Fig. 4). Numerous "events" stipulated by the Leeson–Levin model are missing, but all of the essential thematic components are there, arranged in the stereotypical pattern of tutti–solo contrast, including the cadenza. Even the point of recapitulation is texturally articulated – by a two-bar tutti passage at the end of the development, during which the soloist sustains a right-hand trill; an *Eingang* then connects this trill to the solo recapitulation. Due to a "shortage" of closing themes (and the absence of theme *2*, the *forte* drive to a half-cadence), the ritornello to the cadenza is based on a motive from theme *E*, the solo "coda" theme.

Figure 5 *K. 503, organization of Andante (tutti themes in boldface)*

	RIT.	EXPO.	DEV./RETRANS.	RECAP.	CODA
theme	**1 2 4 6**	**1 2** C 4' E	"E" "2"	**1 2** 4' E	**6** 6
key	I	I V V	V-pedal	I	I

The Andante of K. 503 is another matter entirely (see Fig. 5). This movement also begins with an orchestral ritornello, but once the solo enters it plays almost continuously. There is no cadenza, nor is the sonata structure articulated by ritornellos except at the end, where the semblance of one begins the coda: the orchestra alone plays the "closing" theme 6 and then repeats it with heterophonic decorations by the solo. Except for this brief element of orchestral symmetry – theme 6 used exclusively to close both the opening ritornello and the movement as a whole[18] – one might have been tempted to describe this movement as an accompanied sonata with an orchestral introduction.

The juxtaposition of these two Andantes, K. 414/385p and K. 503, illustrates some commonalities to second-movement concerto form and some of the ways in which it differs from its first-movement counterpart. It also highlights some of the changes that Mozart introduced to the form in his later concertos: the main structural divisions are less likely to be articulated by textural contrast (i.e., ritornellos); the cadenza is abandoned (K. 453 is the last slow movement to have one); and the solo plays more continuously, most conspicuously in the coda. This would explain why Mozart needed only one short closing theme for the ritornello of K. 503. Had he planned to end the movement with a cadenza and a concluding orchestral ritornello, a single closing theme would surely have been insufficient. In important details, the Andante of K. 467 differs from both of these examples, and those differences contribute to its special character. Therefore, while a separate study of slow-movement concerto form is invaluable,[19] first-movement form remains a useful touchstone (see Fig. 6).

The Andante of K. 467 is in the subdominant key of F major, and as in the Romance of K. 466, trumpets and timpani do not participate. The Andante begins with a one-bar "vamp" which establishes the movement's characteristic sonority (muted upper strings, taking full advan-

Figure 6 K. 467/II, organization (tutti themes printed in boldface)

	RITORNELLO				EXPOSITION					DEVELOPMENT							RECAPITULATION					CODA	
	R1				S1							R2			S2								
bar	1	8	12	17	22	23	30	35	37	45	50	55	58	61	62	66	73	79	83	88	94	100	103
theme	**1a**	**1b**	**2**	**6**	**7**	1a	1b	2	**C**	2	6	**X**	**X**	**"7"**	**"C"**	**"2"**	1a	**"1b"**	2	**6**	**1b**	Y	**7**
key	F			(f)		F			F→d→(c)	C		C→g→d→B♭					A♭	→	(f)	F		F	
										=RIT.					=EXPO/RIT.		=RIT.		=EXPO/RIT.	=EXPO.		NEW	≈RIT.

tage of the divided violas, and pizzicato cellos and basses[20]) and sets in motion the throbbing triplets which, except for one magical moment (bars 70–2), animate the entire movement. The bass line of this vamp outlines the tonic triad, a figure common enough in tonal music, but one which constitutes a prominent motivic link among the concerto's three movements (see in particular, in the first movement, bars 108 [flute], 109–10 [piano], 409–10 [winds], and 414–15 [strings]; and in the last movement, bars 58–60 [piano]). This outlined triad is then decorated by the first violins to launch the long, unbroken melody that runs through the entire ritornello. Its serene beginning (Fig. 6: *1a*) hovers high above the pulsating accompaniment and consists of complementary three-bar phrases that end in a full cadence (bar 7), the only one until the end of the ritornello. The continuation (Fig. 6: *1b*), with its large melodic leaps, is a two-step sequence that veers toward the minor and seems directed toward a half-cadence, though the expected dominant chord is replaced by a minor six-four. Another sequence (Fig. 6: *2*) then follows, more uneasy, chromatic and minor-inflected, expressing an emotional ambivalence by simultaneously containing patterns that rise (first bassoon and second violins) and fall (first violins and flute). Built over a dominant pedal, it suggests preparation for the "second theme" but leads instead to a *piano* "closing theme" (Fig. 6: *6*), which restores the major modality and brings relief with its "cleansing," pure diatonic descent. Like theme *1a*, it is in balanced three-bar phrases, though its closing cadence is elided with a modest flourish (Fig. 6: *7*) that descends in its single bar through an F-major arpeggio and is supported by the first root-position tonic chord since bar 7. This flourish thus balances the opening vamp, both harmonically and motivically. In fact, the entire ritornello displays an arch form, with harmonically stable outer pillars (vamp and "first theme" at the beginning, "closing theme" and flourish at the end), separated by two minor-inflected sequences (*1b* and *2*). Notably missing from the design is a tonally stable "second theme."

The solo exposition begins, like the ritornello, with the one-bar vamp, in which the continuous triplets are taken over by the pianist's left hand while the strings outline the accompanying pizzicato triads. The solo then "sings" the opening themes, *1a* and *1b*. The latter, however, is significantly transformed through the negation of the two features that, in the ritornello, might have identified it as a "*forte* drive to a half-cadence": it is now marked *piano* throughout and is extended to a full cadence in the tonic. The leaps in *1b* are now vast, spanning more than three octaves and extending into the instrument's deepest reaches. These modifications, together with the banishment of the minor inflections, lend the theme a purity and tranquility that it lacked in the ritornello.

The orchestra responds with a facsimile of the flourish that had closed the ritornello (*7*). Its appearance here may be compared with the similar introduction, in first-movement form, of the ritornello flourish to acknowledge the tonic cadence that concludes the solo statement of the opening theme, thereby freeing it to modulate. Here, however, the orchestral flourish itself initiates the modulation by cadencing in D minor, in which key the solo begins its episodic "bridge" passage (Fig. 6: *C*) – an ardent cantilena. This solo "episode" theme negates D minor by restoring the tonic, F major, before proceeding to a half-cadence in the dominant key, C major, as if preparing for the "second theme." The return of the original string texture (with the pizzicato bass) at the harmonic turning point in the middle of this episode (bar 41), seems to offer further reassurance that the movement is "on track."

At this point in first-movement form, the solo has the option of presenting as its dominant-key "second theme" either the orchestra's lyric theme from the ritornello (theme *4* in the Leeson–Levin model) or a new theme of its own (theme *D*). In this instance there is no lyrical orchestral theme to adopt, and the possibility of a new solo theme is thwarted when, in bar 44, the orchestra shifts into the minor for theme *2*, which the piano embroiders. The reversion to ritornello themes continues with theme *6*, which restores the major mode and closes the exposition. The piano remains prominent in the presentation of this theme (for its first half it is doubled an octave below by the violins, while for its second the flute joins in at the unison), but in the process it has sacrificed not only an independent second theme (*D*), but its key-confirming coda (*E*). The thematic constitution of the exposition is thus closely modeled on the ritornello. The chief differences are that the flourish (*7*) has been displaced to serve a different function and a solo episode has been added to "thematize" the modulation to the dominant. In each section the harmonic goal is not reached until its final bar, and each lacks a "second theme." While there are obviously precedents for this type of sonata exposition, it is unusual, especially for Mozart.[21] In the present instance it seems to take on a particular significance, contributing simultaneously to the music's floating quality and, quoting Girdlestone, to its "perpetual instability."[22]

There is certainly little time to savor the arrival in the dominant, for the ritornello that follows begins immediately to modulate, thus marking the start of the "development." Textural continuity is promoted through the participation of the piano: a new three-bar tutti theme (Fig. 6: *X*) cadences in G minor and is then repeated by the solo, transposed down a fourth to cadence in D minor. The orchestra dramatically breaks the pattern in bar 61 – the movement's only full bar marked *forte* – and heads toward a cadence in B-flat major as the winds adopt the repeating triplets that they reserve for the flourish (*7*). In the "relaxed" subdominant key of B-flat major the piano presents at bar 62 a radiant new theme which recalls materials previously heard. The phrase structure and the style of both the piano writing and the string accompaniment suggest the episode theme *C*, though the rhythm of the solo melody seems related to *1b*. After only four bars, this brief respite is disturbed by the orchestra, which again initiates a sequence through minor keys, based on *2*. The piano's rising arpeggios in response to each stage of the sequence seem like futile attempts to escape the inexorable downward pull.

The development finally comes to an expectant dominant chord in the home key (bar 71) as if preparing for an orthodox recapitulation – even if the modality is ambiguous. Heightening the sense of anticipation is the relative stillness caused by the sudden cessation of the pulsating triplets – for the only time in the movement. Magically, the winds intervene, a *deus ex machina* offering up harmonies that enable the solo to make an unforeseen escape to the unexpected key of A-flat major, for the beginning of the recapitulation. Eager to get under way, the solo bypasses the "vamp" and immediately launches into the opening theme (*1a*), the beauty and purity of which are enhanced by the fresh key, the rarefied air of the higher register, the delicate embellishments, and the sustaining woodwind halo. This fleeting attainment of sublime beauty sadly brings on a quicker loss as theme *1b* follows (in bar 79), corresponding to its ritornello version but highly transformed: the harmonies immediately veer toward the minor, the winds contribute a doleful countermelody, and the piano melody is broken by rests, its large, yearning leaps replaced by urgent pleading. The sequence of ritornello themes continues with *2* and *6*, essentially in their ritornello forms, but particularly through the presence of the piano, adding features that marked their exposition appearances. There are also some wonderful new touches in the presentation of theme *6*, including new doublings (the plaintive oboe) and the touching addition of the "Lebewohl" motive in the horns (bars 90–1). Since the recapitulation began in A-flat major, the last bar of *6* (bar 93) contains the first strong root-position tonic chord of the entire recapitulation – indeed, the first since the exposition. Thus the tonal shape of the movement as a whole, anchored at the ends and suspended in the middle, reflects the similar pattern of relative harmonic stability presented in microcosm in the opening ritornello. Beginning the recapitulation in a key other than the tonic was therefore essential to this scheme. (For an understanding of why the key of A-flat may have been chosen for this purpose, readers are referred to the Schachter article cited above.)

But the recapitulation is not yet over, as a woodwind *crescendo* in bar 93 encourages the soloist to add a variant of the exposition version of theme *1b*. This "bonus" serves several important functions. Harmonically, it provides a necessary prolongation of the belated arrival in the tonic (analogous to its function in the exposition, where, in contrast, it lent additional harmonic stability to the *opening* theme, *1a*). In keeping with this new closing function, its concluding cadential trill transfers from the leading tone to the supertonic, an apparent allusion to the "absent" theme *E*, which stereotypically closes with a supertonic trill. Structurally, the exposition version of *1b* contributes a sense of thematic completeness, since the earlier return of its ritornello version at bar 79 was so highly disguised. Furthermore, its association with the exposition makes the recapitulation not merely a recasting of the opening ritornello but, as in first-movement form, an integration of both ritornello and exposition features. By virtue of its wide leaps, *1b* is the movement's most striking theme, and it is also the one most subject to transformation and migration: in the ritornello it initiates the "bridge," in the exposition it is part of the "first group," and in the recapitulation it first "corrects" the initial "foreign" tonality and then forms part of the "second group." This pattern of structural displacement and functional reinterpretation was already well established in the first movement.

For the coda, the solo introduces a new triadic theme (Fig. 6: *Y*). The strings meanwhile continue the unison pizzicato accompaniment that they have been contributing since the presentation of theme 6, while the winds now join in with the pulsating triplets characteristic of their flourish (7). The latter is indeed the only ritornello theme still missing from the recapitulation, and though its texture sustains the entire coda the theme itself is withheld until the closing bars (bars 103–4), where the movement finally finds repose in its only *pianissimo* marking. The solo's aspirations are reflected in its ascent (in bars 101 and 104, as earlier in bars 81 and 97) to the very top of the fortepiano keyboard.

The Andante occupies a world apart, a sonic dream world evoked by the magical effect of muted and pizzicato strings. It offers moments of sublime beauty and ends in a state of bliss, but its surface serenity cannot conceal the turmoil that lies beneath. At every turn there is a poignant reminder that happiness is transient, its promise easily revoked. The comparison is banal, to be sure, but as the lovers in *Elvira Madigan* sadly discover, the escape to a dream world is consummated only in the imagination.

5

Finales

The vast majority of Mozart's concerto finales are rondos. Two early concertos – the Piano Concerto in D major, K. 175, and the Violin Concerto in B-flat major, K. 207, both of 1773 – originally had finales in first-movement form, but Mozart subsequently replaced both finales with rondos (K. 382 and K. 269 respectively). The Concertone in C major for two violins, with oboe and cello, K. 190, of 1774 concludes with a minuet, and two piano concertos of the mid-1780s, K. 453 and K. 491, have variation-form finales. However, this handful constitutes the exceptions, and aside from the unique case of the Concertone, Mozart's formal choices were the very options identified by Koch in his *Introductory Essay on Composition*: "The last section of the concerto . . . may take the form of the first allegro, or an ordinary rondo with very amplified episodes, or variations on a short melody consisting of two sections."[1]

In discussions of Mozart's piano concertos, the rondo finales have received far less attention than the first movements. The underlying assumption seems to be that rondo form is relatively unproblematic in comparison with sonata form. This is simply not true. The misleading illusion of relative simplicity and block-like construction is promoted by the widely accepted system of identifying rondo types by alphabetic sequences, such as *ABABA*, *ABACBA*, or *ABACABA* ("textbook" sonata-rondo). Indeed, each of Mozart's piano-concerto finales can be construed as belonging to one of these three categories, though doing so misrepresents the great variety of thematic constructions that the movements actually display and the degree to which sonata style and ritornello structures impact the form. The finale rondos may also exhibit aspects of variation in either the refrains (e.g., K. 449 and K. 451) or the episodes (e.g., K. 382, which could even be categorized as theme and variations). In the face of this wide range of structural

73

options, Joel Galand has suggested that "for 18th-century composers, the rondo was not a strict form but rather a more loosely defined genre which could be adapted to various formal procedures: sectionalized ternary forms, variation, and expanded binary structures."[2] This definition may be a bit broad, but it is a valuable corrective to the opposite extreme, which seeks to pigeonhole the rondo into alphabetic cell-blocks.

A basic problem for the concerto rondo is how to express solo–tutti contrast through the form. Is there a role for ritornellos, for example? One useful function for one would be to set off the cadenza, if there is to be one (which there often is, immediately preceding the final return of the refrain). But this is a unique circumstance. Bearing in mind Tovey's insight that an important function of the orchestral ritornello is to supplement the solo's tonal climax with dynamic force, it stands to reason that a weighty ritornello would be counterproductive following a rondo episode, since the eventual goal of the episode is not to mark an ending but to lead back to the refrain. Therefore, if there are to be ritornellos, or something resembling them, they would more logically be associated with the refrain, which represents the home tonality – either established or regained. In the most extreme case, the ritornello and the rondo refrain might be congruent, played consistently by the orchestra in alternation with solo episodes, as happens, for example, in the finale of Bach's Violin Concerto in E major, BWV 1042, and as is nearly the case in the rondo finale of Mozart's Bassoon Concerto, K. 191/186e. However, in other Mozart concerto finales that begin with an orchestral ritornello (e.g., the Piano Concertos K. 365/316a, K. 413/387a, K. 414/385p, K. 449, K. 451, and K. 503), the subsequent returns of the opening refrain theme are generally introduced by the solo.

Given the piano's habitual role in leading back to and initiating returns of the refrain, it is natural that Mozart explored the option of expressing solo–tutti contrast within the opening refrain, even beginning the movement with a solo presentation of the refrain theme. This gambit is possible in a second or third movement, Tovey would remind us, because the solo and the orchestra have already established a relationship in the first movement. The majority of Mozart's piano-concerto rondo finales are indeed begun by the solo, and Tovey based his *Encyclopaedia Britannica* "definition" of the Classical concerto rondo on just such a model: "In the rondos of classical concertos . . . the orchestra (especially in Mozart) finds its opportunity in a series of accessory themes announced as soon as the solo instrument has given out the rondo-theme. These accessories are then held in reserve for the coda."[3] Tovey described this same scheme somewhat more fully and colorfully in the course of his analysis of K. 488: "The essential feature in the concerto-finale is that the solo player states the theme, and the orchestra gives a counterstatement, to which it appends a long string of other themes, none of which is destined to reappear until the last stages of the work, where they all troop in and make a triumphant end."[4] Obviously there is more to it than this, even in the few details that Tovey describes. Some of the "long string" of themes may find their way into the movement *before* the "last stages." In K. 503, for example, part of the "string" is appended to the first return of the refrain. And in K. 415/387b, the orchestral ritornello not only repeats the piano's opening statement of the rondo theme but, much like a first-movement ritornello, goes on to anticipate the "transition" and "second" themes of the solo "exposition," although its "cadence" theme does not return until the "recapitulation."

Mozart also divides the opening rondo theme between solo and orchestra in a number of different ways besides the "solo statement/tutti counterstatement" formula. Such distributions are facilitated by the very nature of finale themes. As Rosen explains it, "the finale is itself a resolution of the entire work, and demands melodic material that will resist, rather than imply, development." Therefore, "the thematic material of a finale is always rhythmically squarer than that of a first movement, the cadences heavily emphasized, the phrases well-defined, and the first theme completely rounded off before any harmonic movement can take place." "Antiphonal treatment both brings out this character most clearly and colors it most effectively."[5] A number of Mozart's concerto rondo themes are accordingly organized in closed, balanced patterns of four phrases (*aabb*, *aaba*, etc.) and scored in a variety of ways, e.g., solo–tutti–solo–tutti (K. 459), solo–tutti–tutti–solo (K. 537), solo–tutti–solo–solo (K. 482 and K. 595), or tutti–tutti–tutti–solo (K. 467). The solo entry may also be delayed by a substantial tutti (as described above), or, alternatively, the movement may open with an extended solo (K. 271).

K. 466: [Allegro assai]

In the autograph of K. 466, Mozart left behind the fragmentary opening of his first attempt at a finale, which is very different from his definitive version and breaks off after thirty-nine bars.[6] Only the outer string parts are notated – enough, however, to indicate that this version was to have begun with a substantial orchestral tutti. The opening rondo theme is a closed, twenty-four-bar ternary structure (‖: *a* :‖: *ba′* :‖), dominated by obsessive repetitions of its lurching opening motive (see Example 4). No doubt Mozart could have done wonders with this material, but he set it aside, presumably for some future occasion – another D-minor piano concerto, about which we can only dream. In its place he wrote the movement with which we are familiar, and as in the second movement, his afterthought was to let the piano initiate the drama, unaccompanied. It does so impulsively, with the explosion of a high-speed D-minor Mannheim rocket that shatters the mood of the preceding Romance (Fig. 7: *A¹*).

The beginning of the definitive K. 466 finale follows the Tovey formula: a thirteen-bar solo statement of the rondo theme (*A¹*), answered by a seventeen-bar orchestral counterstatement (Fig. 7: *A²*). As the disparity in lengths indicates, this counterstatement is no mere repetition, but departs from the piano's example after only two bars and, through excited sequential and imitative elaborations, ends dramatically on the dominant. There is an obvious parallel here with the first-movement ritornello, where the opening theme (Fig. 1: *1*) also cadenced in the tonic and was followed by a modified *forte* counterstatement which culminated in a half-cadence (Fig. 1: *2*). From this point on, though, resemblances to first-movement ritornello form are minimal. *A³* (at bar 30; see Fig. 7) begins its tense tremolo-driven rising chromatic scale (in two-part imitation) over a sustained dominant pedal, and thus bears some resemblance to a typical half-cadence theme *3* in the Leeson–Levin model. But its second half, which reverses the direction of the chromatic scale (now in *three*-part imitation), is mostly over a tonic pedal and, in the end, resolves deceptively to a submediant (B-flat) chord. The concluding ritornello theme (Fig. 7: *A⁴*) sustains the energy and *forte* dynamic and functions as a closing theme. The overall effect of this chain of ritornello themes (the "refrain complex") is thus markedly different from the

Example 4 K. 466/III, original opening theme

first-movement ritornello model. It may have a prominent half-cadence midpoint break, but its thematic components hardly suggest the rhetoric of a sonata exposition, nor are they differentiated by dynamic contrast. The "refrain complex" is uniformly *forte* and intense, and its themes are both texturally related and motivically linked, contributing to the impression of breathless momentum. Mozart satisfies the principle of thematic economy by bringing back each of these themes later in the movement, but their specific destinies might be difficult to predict: A^2 returns modified at the analogous spot in the recapitulation (offering the semblance of a "recapitulatory tutti"), A^3 appears altered (and in the tonic major) in the coda, and A^4 constitutes the ritornello to the cadenza.

After the hard-driven refrain complex, the solo re-enters, offering lyric contrast with an arresting "new" theme in the tonic (Fig. 7: *E*, the "re-entry theme," at bar 63). In point of fact, *E* is not entirely new. Its opening motive, *a–c♯–d*, has just been heard as the melody of the preceding cadence (bars 61–2).[7] It has also figured not only in the rondo theme (A^1, bar 1), but in principal themes from the first movement: the ritornello "lyric" theme (Fig. 1: *4*, bar 34, in the flute, transposed), the solo "first" theme (Fig. 1: *N*, bars 77–8), and the solo "second" theme (Fig. 1: *D*, bars 128–9, albeit transposed and somewhat modified).[8] Furthermore, *E*'s cadential gesture (bars 72–3) echoes that of A^1 (bars 12–13, though bar 72 is actually identical to bar 9). As if taking its cue from this resemblance, the piano immediately launches into the rondo theme (A^1). After only five bars, however, it transforms that theme into a modulatory passage and, with string accompaniment, culminates in a half-cadence in the relative major, F major – ostensibly on the brink of the second group or, in sonata-rondo terms, the *B* section.

Figure 7 *K. 466/III, organization*

concerto:	**R1**					**S1**								
sonata:	EXPOSITION													
	(first group)							(second group)				(retransition)		
rondo:	*A* (91 bars)							*B* (75 bars)						
bar:	1	13	30	51		63	73	92	110	139/147	154	161	166–167
theme:	A^1	A^2	A^3	A^4		*E*	(A^1)	B^1	B^2	B^3/B^3	codetta	(A^1)	[*Eingang*]
key:	d	d				d	→	f	F	F		→	

concerto:	**R2**		**S2**										**R3**	cadenza
sonata:	RECAPITULATION													
	(first group)		(secondary development)					(second group)						
rondo:	*A* (29 bars)		*C* (75 bars)					*B* (75 bars)						
bar:	167	180	196	206	230	240	264	271	289	302/310	317		337	345
theme:	A^1	(A^2)	*E*	(A^1)	*E*	*E*	(A^1)	B^1	B^2	B^3/B^3	B^2		A^4	cadenza
key:	d	→	a	→	g	d	→	d	d	d	d			

concerto:	**R4** (with solo participation)			
sonata:	"SUMMARIZING" CODA			
rondo:	*A* **Coda** (8 + 75 bars)			
bar:	346	354/363	370	395
theme:	A^1	B^3/B^3	(A^3)	(B^3)
key:	d	D	D	D

Parentheses indicate variants of themes. Tutti themes are shown in boldface.

This pattern of a new re-entry theme (*E*) followed by a modulation based on the rondo theme (*A¹*) is also found in the finales of the adjacent piano concertos, K. 459 and K. 467. In those works, however, the return of the rondo theme prior to the transition is stated by the orchestra, whereas in K. 466 the solo does it all, with breathless intensity. The effect is to give the solo an independent presence and identity in the tonic key *after* the ritornello, and then make it the dramatic agent for the modulation to the new key, in this case the relative major. The juxtaposition of the re-entry and rondo themes will have far-reaching consequences for the rest of the movement. At the same time it points up a parallel with the concerto's first movement, especially striking given the motivic relationship, described above, between the finale's re-entry theme (*E*) and the first movement's solo entry theme (*N*). In the solo exposition of the first movement this new theme (*N*) was also succeeded by the movement's opening theme (*1*), and in both movements the "development" section juxtaposes the two themes. Generalizing beyond K. 466, we may see in the concerto rondo's customary "new" re-entry theme the counterpart to the option, in first-movement form, of beginning the solo exposition with a new theme.

Though its sonata-style transition may have made the appropriate preparation for the expected relative major, F major, the solo is unable to shake the tyranny of the minor modality, and its first utterance is an angry protest in F minor (Fig. 7: B^1, at bar 92). But for its modality, we would take it for the "second theme." The six-bar solo antecedent phrase is answered by an extended thirteen-bar consequent that has the winds taking over the theme, which the pianist embroiders with decorative passagework. During the extension the flute plays, three times, a transposition (c–e–f) of the three-note motive (a–$c\sharp$–d) that had launched the re-entry theme. Shortly before its conclusion, B^1 turns to and cadences in F major, which becomes the point of departure for the next theme, B^2 (at bar 110). B^2 seems to flow directly from B^1, sustaining its energy and adopting its serpentine turn figure (compare bars 112 and 114 of B^2 with bars 102ff of B^1). B^2 also makes allusion, in bars 118–20, to the "rocket" of A^1. It has many of the hallmarks of a first-movement solo "coda" theme: it is in two parts, each driven by vigorous sequences and each ending in a decisive full cadence marked by left-hand Alberti figuration and a right-hand trill on the supertonic – the normative signals of solo closure in first-movement form. However, while these gestures are clearly suggestive of the solo climax, the music itself lacks the momentum actually to deliver it. Of course, it is questionable whether such a climax would even be appropriate, since the fate of rondo B themes is not to present a shattering climax in the dominant (or in this case the relative major), but to return to the A theme and the tonic key. One may therefore hear the piano, in B^2, as coyly pulling back from a kind of conclusion that it recognizes to be inappropriate.

What is undeniable, though, is that by sonata standards the solo has failed to provide a satisfactory second theme. The orchestra recognizes this shortcoming and fills the breach. After a bar of string vamp, the winds introduce a new theme in F major (Fig. 7: B^3), the lyrical "payoff" of the entire section – a buoyant theme whose *buffo* character makes it a true avenue of "escape" out of the prevailing tragedy. The piano embraces the suggestion with alacrity. It repeats the theme and then adds a codetta, using (in bars 154, 156, and 158) the serpentine turn figure that binds the three *B* themes into a unit. Significantly, the piano's left-hand accompaniment for B^3 lacks the bass line, which is supplied by the lower strings. The harmonic "rootlessness" of the solo part both enhances the theme's buoyancy and symbolizes the solo's dependence on the orchestra for access to the *buffo* option (unless Mozart expected the pianist to double the orchestral basses on a pedal-board mechanism, a possibility explored in Chapter 6). After the cadence of the B^3 codetta (bar 160), the solo effects the retransition using the arpeggiated "rocket" figuration of the rondo theme to prefigure and thus prepare for the tonic return of A^1, which arrives in bar 167 following an *Eingang*. Throughout the movement, variants of the rondo theme serve as transitions and retransitions, thereby according that theme a potential for instability that, by contrast, gives its periodic tonic returns an enhanced, even exhilarated feeling of restoration.

The refrain complex is here presented in an abbreviated and open-ended form – by A^1 and a modified A^2. In response to the solo restatement of the entire rondo theme (A^1, bars 167–80), the orchestral counterstatement (A^2) is now far more agitated: impetuous imitative entries of the rondo motive begin at once, the violins become syncopated, and the passage drives to a half-cadence in A minor, the minor dominant, ending with four urgent "hammer blows." As Figure 7 indicates, the solo section that follows ($S2$, bars 196–336) is thematically parallel to the first solo, with some important differences and, obviously, a different tonal trajectory: while the first, "expository" solo ($S1$) modulated from D minor to F major, the second starts in A minor and restores the home tonic, D minor. It begins, like $S1$, with the re-entry theme (E), followed by a transition based on the rondo theme (A^1). The latter, however, is considerably transformed in a manner suggestive of "development," with added sequential wind statements of the rondo motive, and it ends in a dramatic half-cadence in the subdominant, G minor (bars 228–9). As in the preceding orchestral counterstatement (bars 194–5), this half-cadence arrival is marked by four dramatic "hammer blows" and analogously elicits a second solo statement of the re-entry theme, beginning in G minor but extended to cadence in D minor. A third statement of the re-entry theme then follows (bar 240), now in the tonic but still suggesting "development," with the winds and the piano engaging in a quasi-imitative dialogue that gives rise to an extensive "cat-and-mouse" sequence. When this sequence reaches the dominant of D minor, a transposition of the concluding bars of the "exposition bridge" prepares for the return of the B themes in the tonic, D minor (compare bars 264–70 with bars 85–91).

From a sonata-rondo perspective, this first half of $S2$ (bars 196–270) constitutes the developmental C episode, though its ending bypasses the "textbook" return of the rondo refrain in favor of the B section, producing an $ABACBA$ thematic design – in other words, a sonata-rondo with a suppressed or bypassed A. But describing the form this way is misleading, because when the B themes do enter they are precisely what is expected. It is only with respect to a preconceived (and wrong-headed) notion of the form, and not as a result of the musical events actually experienced, that something may seem to have been omitted, suppressed, or bypassed.[9] From a purely sonata-form perspective (viewing the form as a sonata without development) this C section may be regarded as the "secondary development" – the expansion, shortly after the start of the recapitulation, of some of the exposition material that had originally followed the "first theme" (i.e., bars 63–91). As is characteristic of secondary developments, this section emphasizes the subdominant in order to reinforce the tonic resolution.[10]

The recapitulatory B section follows in the tonic, but not without telling changes – melodic, harmonic, and structural. To start with, the altered tonal context completely changes the way in which B^1 is perceived. In its initial appearance it had had an effect of angry protest by turning to F *minor* after F *major* had been prepared. Now, however, we are prepared for D minor, and that is what we get. This makes B^1 more plausible as a "second theme," in the present context, and produces a feeling less of protest than of crushing inevitability. In the consequent phrase the flute is initially replaced by an oboe to produce a more plaintive orchestral sonority, and the rewritten piano figuration struggles to surmount the wind melody rather than merely support it (compare bars 277–80 with bars 98–101). In its earlier appearance, B^1 had cadenced in the major, but now it remains in the tonic minor, a difference that the solo dramatizes with a tense, chromatic tremolo figure (bars 285–7). B^2 then follows in D minor, intensified through the continuous activity of the soloist's two hands but coming to an early end after only its first cadential trill. The orchestral response with B^3 is thus premature, and it hovers between minor and major, as if unable to deny its essential *buffo* character and unwilling to capitulate entirely to the tragic minor-key destiny dictated both by sonata style and the actual proceedings. The piano repeats this version of B^3 and then settles the modal ambiguity decisively in favor of the minor by resuming B^2, whose second half is presented, far more emphatically and in D minor, to seal the fate of the B group. To heighten the excitement, the concluding cadence is considerably extended and dramatized. Taking a cue from the earlier chromatic addition to B^1 (bars 285–7), the piano now offers an even longer and more thrilling chromatic ascent, rising in ever increasing and ever more treacherous leaps to the highest note on Mozart's fortepiano (bars 329–34). The concluding cadential trill is also doubled in length, providing a fitting climax to what has gone before.

Mozart's rearrangement and recasting of the B themes thus gives this section more the character and thrust of its counterpart in first-movement form. The motivation for the change derives from the particular nature of the concerto rondo: while the first B section leads back to the tonic for a solo return of A, the second culminates in the pre-cadenza ritornello. Mozart's reworking of the B themes thus creates conditions propitious for this ritornello, which charges in, *forte*, with the first appearance of trumpets and timpani since the opening ritornello. Drawn from ritornello theme A^4, it ends with the cadential six-four that announces the cadenza. Mozart's cadenza for this movement is unfortunately not extant, but one by Beethoven is. A number of pianists who adopt Beethoven's cadenza for the first movement shun the one for the third. This is a pity. As I have argued elsewhere, Beethoven's cadenzas for K. 466 are "satisfying precisely because they are *echt* Beethoven and not *ersatz* Mozart," which is what we usually get.[11] As in his first-movement cadenza, Beethoven here offers a developmental juxtaposition of the two "first themes" (the rondo and re-entry themes) – a musical and historical extrapolation of Mozart's own "development" section.

After the cadenza, the piano offers the rondo theme (A^1) one last time, but, unwilling to face the consequences of the looming tragic close, it stops short on an expectant harmony. The orchestral winds fill the void and offer a way out: a D-major statement of the *buffo* B^3 theme, the sole theme from the B section that had resisted complete minor-mode assimilation. The solo adopts this theme in turn, a decision that the orchestra applauds with a boisterous diatonic major-mode transformation of ritornello theme A^3, the only ritornello theme that has not yet had a rehearing. Giddy with delight, B^3 returns once more, newly reorganized into balanced two-bar units of alternating tonic and dominant harmonies and culminating in exultant brass fanfares (bars 401–2, 409–10 etc.), which dominate the rest of the movement and bring it to a jubilant close. It is only in its last appearance that the *buffo* theme is played by the orchestra and the solo in concert – the winds singing the melody, the piano providing active accompanimental figuration, and the strings first doubling the bass line and then, on the repeat, adding to the harmonic filler. The *buffo* theme thus becomes the symbolic vehicle for the reconciliation of solo and orchestra, representing the mutually beneficial acceptance of the social order by the individual and the embrace of the individual by society. Wye J. Allanbrook has compared this "comic close" to the "happy endings of Mozart's operas": "a celebration of the social man, of reconciliation, and of accommodation to the way things are."[12] The post-cadenza section is the region where complete solo–tutti integration finally occurs, the culmination of a progressive transcendence of ritornello "control" which may be traced throughout the three movements, finally resulting in a breakdown of the rigid separation of tutti and solo. This section is also where the movement's thematic essence is distilled, a fine example of Mozart's "summarizing coda": a "condensed reprise" or third "rotation" through the principal themes of the primary and secondary groups (A^1 and B^3), to which is added a ritornello theme (A^3) that enhances the sense of closure by virtue of having been withheld until this point.[13]

The plan of the finale in Figure 7 offers three synoptic views of the movement, from the perspectives of concerto, sonata, and rondo (i.e., sonata–rondo) form. Of these, the rondo model (*ABACBA*) is the most problematic. For reasons offered above, it seems misleading to describe it as a sonata–rondo with an omitted *A* section. And the alternative, to conceive the concluding section (*BA*) as a "recapitulation in reverse" seems equally artificial, especially in view of the intervening cadenza.[14] The concerto-based ritornello structure is persuasive, especially considering Mozart's sense of thematic economy in finding precisely one subsequent function for each of the three orchestral ritornello themes (A^2, A^3 and

A^4). The fact that the piano participates throughout much of the final ritornello makes this analysis no less convincing; indeed, I would argue that this integration is an essential part of the design. The sonata model is also apt, much more so than the sonata-rondo model, if we view the finale as a sonata without development (so-called "slow-movement" or "sonatina" form) but with an extensive secondary development and a "summarizing coda." This design, which John Daverio labels "amplified binary" and Joel Galand calls "expanded binary," is one of which Mozart was very fond – as was Brahms. Figure 7 shows the close thematic correspondence between the "exposition" and the "recapitulation," even with some substitutions: the latter part of the orchestral ritornello being replaced by the secondary development, the retransition by the ritornello to the cadenza, and the *Eingang* by the cadenza. As in the earlier movements, the finale's power and intensity are in no small part a function of its formal regularity. In the end, though, it is only by breaking this order, as literally happens in the coda (bar 353), that tragedy is averted and transcendence achieved.

K. 467: Allegro vivace assai

In contrast to the finale of K. 466, that of K. 467 is a true sonata-rondo. Another difference is that the orchestra, not the solo, begins the movement. The solo does, however, participate in the rondo theme (Figure 8: A^1), a ternary form (or three-part song form) – ‖: a :‖ ba ‖ – but the tutti–solo distribution of phrases is quite unusual and unexpected. As Charles Rosen describes it: "The main theme, which begins in the orchestra, ends with a repetition of its first phrase, and this phrase, which now rounds off the melody, is surprisingly played, not by the orchestra, but by the piano; so the soloist both finishes what the orchestra began, and also begins exactly as the orchestra did. This is a pun based on the nature of concerto form."[15] Another result of this melodic structure is that the a phrase, since it serves as both a beginning and an ending, may stand for the entire rondo theme, which actually happens later in the movement. Although orchestra and soloist enter separately but equally with this same phrase, in this initial stage of the finale, as in first-movement form, the former is the initiator and the latter the follower – and a reluctant one at that. The orchestra's b phrase undergoes a

Figure 8 *K. 467/III, organization*

concerto:	**R1**						**S1**							
rondo:	A (109 bars)									B (68 bars)				
bar:	1	28	34	41	46	52	58	75	83	110	120	154	169	177
theme:	A^1	A^2	A^3	A^4	A^5	A^6	**E**	A^1	(A^1)	B^1	B^1 ext	B^2	retransition	[*Eingang*
phrase:	a a b a							a'						
key:	C						C			→ G				→ (V/C)

concerto:	**S1** (contd)	**R2**					**S2**				**R3**
rondo:	A (62 bars)						C (74 bars)				
bar:	178	202	207	213	219	234	240				308
theme:	A^1	A^4	A^3	A^2	A^3 ext	(A^4)	("development" based on A^1)				(A^4)
phrase:	a a b										
key:	C			→ A	A		→		→	→	C

concerto:	**R3** (contd)			**S3**		**R4**			cadenza
rondo:	A (47 bars)					B (64 bars)			
bar:	314	321	327	333		361	371	405 418	424
theme:	A^1	A^3	A^5	**E**	secondary dev.	B^1	B^1 ext	B^2 $(A^6?)$	cadenza
phrase:	a								
key:	C			C	→	C			

concerto:	**S4**
rondo:	A (23 bars)
bar:	425
theme:	A^1
phrase:	a a + ext
key:	C

Parentheses indicate variants of themes; "ext" refers to an extension based on the theme identified. Tutti themes are shown in boldface.

87

pronounced dynamic shift from *piano* to *forte* as it moves toward a dramatic and expectant half-cadence, on which the solo enters with an improvised *Eingang* before proceeding to the concluding *a* phrase. In other words, the solo does not jump in unexpectedly to steal the stage. Rather, the orchestra exhorts, even commands the solo to enter to complete the rondo theme – as if the presence of the piano were required for the theme to continue. To be sure, the *Eingang* allows the piano an opportunity for free expression, to determine the precise nature of its entrance, but this merely delays the moment when it must adopt the orchestra's melody. As in the first movement, the solo must be coaxed to enter. Its natural home seems to be the dream world of the Andante second movement, described by Maynard Solomon as that "floating world far removed from reality."[16] But in the outer Allegros it must join the "real" world, and does so with reluctance – though once it gets underway it is garrulous and irrepressible.

Before the solo embarks on this adventure, however, the orchestra completes the refrain complex with a string of ritornello themes. Quite different from those of the K. 466 finale, these themes are relatively short, quasi-independent blocks, though obviously arranged in a logical progression. A^2 and A^3 form a pair and are varied to produce the corresponding pair A^4 and A^5 (see Figure 8). A^4 superimposes imitative wind statements of the main rondo motive on top of A^2 and, marked *piano*, is the only section of dynamic contrast in this portion of the ritornello. A^6 is the cadential phrase, charging up and down the C-major scale and ending with a unison dotted-figure tattoo. Despite the compelling "line" that connects these themes, they resemble the interchangeable phrases of a musical dice-game, whose order is randomly determined. And, indeed, this is how Mozart seems to treat them later in the movement. This apparent capriciousness in thematic order is one of the sources of delight in this movement, and it is a feature shared by all three movements of K. 467: in the outer Allegros the effect is of high spirits and high play, while in the Andante it is sheer magic. Also linking the outer Allegros is the great number of themes generated by their respective opening motives, contributing further to the impression of an active imagination and a superabundance of creative energy.

As in K. 466 and many other Mozart rondo finales, the solo resumes with a "new" tonic re-entry theme (Fig. 8: *E*), having both immediate and long-range connections with what has gone before. Its bold arpeggiated rise through the notes of the tonic triad retraces in reverse order the cadential scalar descent of the concluding ritornello theme (A^6), providing a compelling local linkage. This stark arpeggio figure is, moreover, the chief motivic link connecting the three movements, appearing most prominently as the G-minor "transition" theme of the first movement (Fig. 2: *C*, bars 109–10) and, in decorated form, as the opening theme of the Andante. Spurred on by horn imitations of this arpeggio motive (bars 60–2 and 64–6),[17] the re-entry theme cadences in the tonic, and the orchestra reinforces this arrival with the cadential portion of the rondo theme (bars 5–8, equivalent to bars 25–8), played first by the strings and repeated by the winds (bars 74–82). The solo then converts this rondo theme into a sonata-style transition. The foreign key that it seems to be preparing, however, is the minor dominant, G minor – a nod toward the G-minor transition theme from the first movement (Figure 2: *C*), to which the finale's re-entry theme is motivically linked. At the very last moment, however, the piano reverses the feint and slips lightheartedly into the orthodox major dominant, to the apparent delight of the winds, which introduce the antecedent phrase of the jovial theme (Fig. 8: B^1, bar 110) marking the beginning of the "second group" and the start of the rondo's *B* section. With encouragement from the strings, the solo takes up this theme and, with flurries of scalar passagework, extends its consequent phrase to a cadence.[18] The solo then introduces theme B^2 (bar 154), which functions as a cadence theme.

A retransition and *Eingang* lead to the return of the rondo refrain, introduced by the piano with string accompaniment. The solo–tutti distribution of the rondo theme is altered for this appearance – to solo statement followed by tutti repetition – which is precisely what one might have expected at the start of the movement. Clearly, the solo has come into its element. Its continuation of the theme is also altered. After eight bars of the *b* phrase, it bypasses the dramatic half-cadence gesture (of bars 17–20) and instead rounds out the rondo theme with two of the "interchangeable" ritornello themes from the refrain complex: A^4 (but stripped of the A^2 countermelody), followed by A^3 (which it decorates and shares with the winds). An orchestral ritornello then rounds out the refrain, or at least begins to do so by launching into its original series of ritornello themes: A^2 and A^3. Theme A^3, however, halts its sequential progression on the submediant harmony and, in stages separated by bar-long rests, establishes this new key (A minor). As in the approach to the *B* section, however, a modal shift carries us into the major (A major) with a threefold statement of the opening motive of the rondo theme, resembling A^4 though differently harmonized. This orchestral ritornello, a reworking of the refrain complex, is thus comparable to the middle ritornello in first-movement form, which rounds out the solo exposition and leads to the second solo (the "development"). The nature of rondo form, however, dictates that this ritornello be attached not to the solo exposition, but to the rondo refrain.

The *C* episode that follows resembles a sonata development. It is based almost entirely on variants of the rondo theme and contains considerable dialogue between the piano and the winds, initially to create a new thematic structure in A major (bars 240–65), and then to travel through two sequences, first through minor keys in two-bar exchanges (bars 277–89) and then through major keys in alternating single bars (bars 289–94). As has become the pattern in this movement, the retransition threatens a minor-key resolution, using, in bars 301–7, the half-step returning-tone figure from the opening ritornello of the *first* movement (bars 44–6). C major is restored, however, in bars 308–13, by precisely the same material (a variant of A^4) that had established A major at the start of the *C* episode. In other words, the "development" is both entered and exited via the same six-bar thematic block by means of which the orchestra turns minor into major.

The returns of the rondo refrain are becoming progressively more concise, contributing to the feeling of increasing excitement and breathlessness. This second return is probably the minimum needed to suggest a refrain complex: the *a* phrase of A^1 played by the solo, answered by the orchestra with A^3 and A^5. The pattern of textural contrast at this juncture is comparable to the first movement of the Piano Concerto in F major, K. 459, which has a brief tutti making the retransition to the recapitulation, and a solo statement of the opening theme followed by a tutti restatement.

The solo re-entry theme (*E*) at bar 333, eager to get underway, is now elided with the end of the ritornello and becomes the basis for an exciting secondary development. In bar 339, in place of the horns' expected second imitation of the theme's bold triadic opening, the motive instead passes from strings to bassoons, where, to thrilling effect, it appears in diminution to help drive the re-entry theme through a pattern of descending thirds: first to A minor, then to F major, the same sequence of keys explored in the development (bars 266–79). In bar 351 this secondary development merges with the exposition transition theme (compare bars 351–8 with bars 102–9), though now heading toward the tonic for the "recapitulation" of the B themes. Once again, a minor-key resolution is threatened and thwarted. The onset of the B section is delayed, however, by two added bars of woodwind transition (bars 359–60), which allow the solo a moment to catch its breath before taking up B^1. In the expository B section this theme had been introduced by the orchestra, but now the solo takes the lead, a sign of its increasing authority as the movement unfolds. The extended consequent phrase of B^1 is likewise rescored, with the theme in the winds and running passagework in the piano, leading to the closing B^2. In comparison with their "exposition" counterparts, these B themes contain felicitous melodic, harmonic, and registral adjustments too numerous to detail. Some changes result from Mozart's need to keep the transposed passagework within the compass of the fortepiano keyboard while still using the full upper range to brilliant effect. Other changes respond to intervening events, such as the recasting of bars 128–33 in bars 379–84 to replicate the sequence pattern of descending thirds – through C-major, A-minor, and F-major harmonies – that had just been presented in the secondary development. In the closing B^2 theme, the solo melody in bars 408–10 is given a new chromatic profile that resembles the main rondo motive, while the wind answer (bars 413–17) has both a new melody and more poignant harmonies, to which the piano adds active running scales. In bar 418 the full orchestra enters *forte*, countermanding the closure of B^2 with a ritornello that culminates in a cadential six-four chord to signal the start of the cadenza. Melodically, this ritornello continues the chromatic line begun by the soloist in bars 408–10, while adding two motives reminiscent of ritornello theme A^6 (the only theme not yet recalled): the violin anacrusis in bar 418 calls to mind bar 52, while the flute in bars 418–19 and the trumpet and timpani in bars 420–1 reproduce the dotted figure of bars 56–7.

Following the cadenza, the piano presents its final, playful statement of the rondo refrain, which is now distilled to its essence: the *a* phrase.

The strings provide accompaniment, a favor which the piano returns when they respond with the same lighthearted phrase. Its closing cadence is then echoed – first by the strings, then by the winds, and finally by the full orchestra – as the piano continues spiritedly with a series of rising scales. Despite the solo's subsidiary, non-thematic role in these closing bars, the impression of a closing ritornello is undermined by several factors: the delay of the *forte* dynamic until the final two bars, the absence of the auxiliary ritornello themes from the refrain complex, and the piano's continuous virtuosic activity. Although the piano does not dominate the conclusion, it has nevertheless established its presence and earned a position of respectability within the social order. It abandons all soloistic posturing, and the orchestra in turn becomes less domineering, producing a satisfying sense of textural and formal integration.

6

Performance practice issues

Performance practice issues are relevant to any musical repertory, but they take on a heightened significance in relation to the Classical piano concerto.[1] Since the very definition of concerto form hinges on the opposition of two unequal forces, the solo and the orchestra, any factor that alters the "balance of power" between them naturally influences the perception of the form. The use of "historical" as opposed to "modern" instruments for both solo and orchestra, combined with "historically informed" decisions with respect to the number of orchestral players and their seating arrangement, represent merely some of the most obvious "hardware" choices that contribute both to the quantitatively measured balance between the forces and to the quality of their sonic contrast.

The pianist's historically grounded option to embellish melodies, particularly in slow movements, may also add expressive force and prominence to the solo line, especially in contrast with the simpler style of orchestral utterances. Additionally, decisions regarding the cadenzas can contribute to the perception of the soloist's personality and stance with respect to the concerto. A performer can obviously display virtuosity and individuality by playing Mozart's own cadenzas (when they are extant) but may make an even more individualistic impression by improvising (or precomposing) cadenzas or by choosing cadenzas written by others. A cadenza that eschews the Mozartian model may introduce a stylistically foreign element to the work, thereby accentuating the sense in which the cadenza is a structural element supplementary to the form. On the other hand, a cadenza in a pseudo–Mozart style may have the opposite effect, supporting a stylistic consistency and continuity between the cadenza and the movement of which it is a part. Another historically justifiable solo responsibility is the option to play continuo

93

during the tuttis and the orchestral portions of the solo sections. This, too, can alter the perceived balance and relationship between solo and tutti. If the continuo consists merely of discreet chordal support, the piano may seem, in the solo sections, to emerge as an individual "voice" from within the ensemble. If, on the other hand, the figured bass is realized with strikingly independent melodic or rhythmic materials that vie with the orchestra for the listener's attention, the piano's autonomy will be made audibly explicit from the outset, though somewhat kept in check until the unrestrained, fully independent (and typically unaccompanied) utterance that launches the first solo. Finally, if the pianist declines to play continuo, the separation of the opposing forces is amplified, and the anticipation of the solo entrance takes on greater dramatic significance. These alternative treatments of the basso continuo may likewise suggest different social models to critics fond of personifying musical interactions.

Subtle psychological aspects of the balance between soloist and orchestra may also be influenced by a soloist's decision to dispense with the conductor and direct the performance from the keyboard, as was Mozart's practice. With a conductor on the podium presiding over the orchestra, there is the sense of a singular personality or agent not only directing but representing, and even personifying, the orchestra in juxtaposition to the soloist. Admittedly, the particular dynamic is very much a function of the actual individuals involved – not only their musical persuasiveness, but their personal charisma and, for better or worse, the relative magnitude of their reputations. Is it a deferential Carlo Maria Giulini accommodating Vladimir Horowitz, an obedient Cord Garben yielding to Arturo Benedetti Michelangeli, an indulgent Kurt Masur proudly showing off the child prodigy of the moment, or is it more of a partnership like that achieved by Colin Davis and Stephen Kovacevich or Adolf Busch and Rudolf Serkin? In contrast, when the pianist also leads the orchestra a different dynamic is set in motion. The opposed forces tend to be perceived as two separate but interwoven elements emanating from a single agent, who both contributes sounds and directs "others" to do so. This was very much the case when Leonard Bernstein conducted the Vienna Philharmonic from the keyboard, though perhaps less so when Murray Perahia coached and directed the malleable and responsive but essentially self-sufficient English Chamber Orchestra. In the latter instance, the effect, reinforced by the intimacy and subtlety of the pianist's approach, is perhaps more suggestive of large-scale chamber music. A curious middle ground is occupied by the democratic and conductorless Orpheus Chamber Orchestra, which, when collaborating with a soloist, projects a personality without a persona.

The performance that looms largest in the imagination is one that we can never experience: Mozart's own, with the composer himself as both soloist and conductor for an audience that was hearing the work for the first time. The impression of experiencing, if not exactly a re-creation of the compositional act, then at least a symbolic reenactment of it would have been enhanced by Mozart's improvisation of embellishments, cadenzas, and figured bass. Such "additions" blur the line between composition and performance, especially since the audience at the première would have had difficulty distinguishing what had been composed from what was being improvised. While "original" instruments may help to recapture some of the purely acoustical qualities of eighteenth-century performances, it is rather through these sorts of improvised contributions that modern pianists can most effectively re-create the atmosphere of spontaneity that probably characterized those "original" performances. On the other hand, we must never forget that the impression of spontaneity is a function of *how* music is played, not of the notes themselves. Furthermore, spontaneity is probably not the most important musical value.

Improvised embellishment

A variety of evidence – from treatises, period testimony, and musical sources – suggests that Mozart and his contemporaries routinely embellished their performances of solo music, including concertos. Precisely *how* they did so remains somewhat elusive, though we have a number of clues. Closest to home, for Mozart at least, is Chapter Eleven of Leopold Mozart's *Treatise on the Fundamental Principles of Violin Playing* (1756), devoted to "the Tremolo, Mordent, and some other improvised Embellishments." Even more extensive treatments of the subject are contained in two influential treatises on keyboard playing: Carl Philipp Emanuel Bach's *Essay on the True Art of Playing Keyboard Instruments* (1753 and 1762), whose second chapter deals with

"Embellishments," and Daniel Gottlob Türk's *School of Clavier Playing* (1789), whose fifth chapter is "Concerning Extemporaneous Ornamentation." The latter offers an instructive example of what *not* to do (apply a turn or trill to every other note) but, more important, an extended model illustrating "how to follow the rules which have been given."[2] The information contained in these and other treatises has been culled, evaluated, and applied to the music of Mozart by Frederick Neumann in *Ornamentation and Improvisation in Mozart* (1986). Like Eva and Paul Badura-Skoda in *Interpreting Mozart on the Keyboard* (1957, trans. 1962), Neumann echoes the eighteenth-century treatises in advising performers to exercise caution and restraint in adding embellishments, but such warnings are hardly necessary today, when improvised embellishment is still the exception rather than the rule and when even the most extravagant of modern embellishers sounds inhibited in comparison with what we know was possible within eighteenth-century practice.

Testimony describing Mozart's embellishment of his piano concertos is surprisingly slim, in addition to being second-hand, posthumous, and of questionable reliability. The most tantalizing report was not published until 1840, in F. X. Schnyder von Wartensee's encyclopedia entry for two amateur-musician brothers, Philipp Karl and Heinrich Anton Hoffmann.[3] The brothers heard Mozart perform two of his piano concertos, K. 459 and K. 537, in Frankfurt on 15 October 1790, and shortly thereafter the composer visited them in Mainz, where he played a violin sonata in A major (either K. 305 or K. 526) with Heinrich Anton, and the Four-Hand Piano Sonata in F major, K. 497, with Philipp Karl. The latter reported that when Mozart played the slow movements of his piano concertos he embellished them "tenderly and tastefully once one way, once differently following the momentary inspiration of his genius."[4] In 1803 he published embellished versions of six Mozart piano concerto slow movements (K. 467, K. 482, K. 488, K. 491, K. 503, and K. 595), presumably inspired by his contact with Mozart but not imitative of the composer's own improvisations. Indirect substantiation of Hoffmann's report comes from Friedrich Rochlitz's often unreliable "Authentic Anecdotes from Wolfgang Gottlieb Mozart's Life," serialized in the *Allgemeine musikalische Zeitung* between 1798 and 1801. The thirteenth anecdote (printed 21 November 1798) described Mozart's performance of the Piano Concertos, K. 456 and K. 503, in Leipzig on 12 May 1789. According to Rochlitz, Mozart played "from a piano part which had a peculiar appearance. It contained nothing except a figured bass, over which were written out only the main ideas; the figures, passages and such things were only lightly indicated. He could presume to do this because he could rely as much on his memory as on his feeling."[5] One possible interpretation is that when "feeling" took over from "memory," improvised embellishment came into play. Maynard Solomon connects Rochlitz's anecdote with a comment in Franz Xaver Niemetschek's 1798 Mozart biography: "As his works were in unbelievable demand, he was never quite sure whether a new work of his, even while it was being copied, had not been stolen. So he generally wrote only a line for one hand in his piano concertos and played the rest from memory." These remarks do not address the issue of improvisation, implying instead that Mozart relied on his memory when playing from a score that was fully "composed" but incompletely notated.

There is little musical source material to substantiate or clarify the Rochlitz and Niemetschek accounts: no such shorthand drafts of the concertos have been uncovered, although, as Solomon points out, the left hand of the piano part is lacking in parts of the autograph of the "Coronation" Concerto, K. 537. Instances of "incomplete notation" may be found in other piano concerto autographs as well, but generally where patterns have been established in the passagework and Mozart uses a shorthand to indicate their continuation (even if the specifics of that continuation are not always obvious).[6] The autograph of the Piano Concerto in C Minor, K. 491, however, might offer some support for Rochlitz's recollection, even though this is not one of the concertos mentioned in the anecdote. Throughout much of this score, the solo part (and particularly the right hand) appears initially to have been only lightly notated and, in places, barely sketched. At a subsequent compositional stage, Mozart used heavier pen strokes to darken, complete, and, when so moved, revise the sketchy notation. This two-stage process is particularly apparent where the final version differed so substantially from the initial sketch that it was entered not in the piano part, which was crossed out, but on blank adjacent staves. Mozart logged the concerto in his personal catalogue, indicating 24 March 1786 as the date of completion, and he performed it two weeks later, on 7 April. It is certainly possible, then, that he played from the score when the solo part was still in a sketch stage[7] (much as Rochlitz described it, with "only the main ideas" written out and "the figures, passages and such things . . . only lightly indicated"), and that he fixed the details of the solo part after the première. This argument, of course, would hardly apply to the two concertos named in the Rochlitz anecdote, since they were completed five and three years, respectively, before the performance in question. Nevertheless, the autograph of K. 491 may still shed light on the possibility of Mozart's improvisation in performance. In bars 41–88 of the finale, the autograph contains for some passages as many as four versions, the "final" one of which is lightly sketched and, in some details, incompletely notated; furthermore, in bar 44 *all* versions are crossed out, challenging the notion that a "definitive" solo part even exists. While this in itself does not prove that Mozart improvised embellishments, it does indicate that the autograph score cannot tell us precisely what Mozart played when he performed this concerto. On the other hand, the existence of so many revised drafts within the autograph shows that he was not indifferent to the detailed working out of material that a lesser composer might have treated casually as formulaic passagework.[8]

Further documentary testimony, also supported by a musical source, is contained in a letter of 9 and 12 June 1784, in which Mozart wrote that his sister "is quite right in saying that that there is something missing in the solo passage in C in the Andante of the concerto in D [K. 451]." He thus promised to "supply the deficiency as soon as possible" and send her the missing decorations together with the cadenzas, which she had also requested.[9] An embellished version of this passage (bars 56–62) contained in a set of manuscript parts found in a Salzburg monastery may represent the very decorations that Mozart presumably sent to his sister. It has thus often been presented as a model for decorating similarly "bare" passages in concerto slow movements.[10] Rudolf Serkin, on the other hand, considered its very existence evidence that "any change from the manuscript was an exception." If it was customary to deviate from the autograph, he argued, Nannerl "could easily have played her own variant."[11] The latter point is surely true, but she probably believed – and no doubt rightly – that her brother could do it better. It would have been the same with her request for the cadenzas: she recognized that they were needed but missing from the score, realized that she needed to include them in her performances, perhaps had doubts about her own improvisatory or compositional skills, and certainly knew that the ones her brother could supply would be superior to her own.

Another musical source, more extensive and more problematic, is a decorated version of the Adagio of the Piano Concerto in A major, K. 488, which Wolfgang Plath attributed to Barbara Ployer, the pupil for whom Mozart wrote the Piano Concertos, K. 449 and K. 453.[12] This document may profitably be considered in conjunction with the embellished versions of Mozart's piano concertos that were published in the early nineteenth century: not only Philipp Karl Hoffmann's "elaborations" of six slow movements, mentioned above, but ornamented editions of entire concertos by John Baptist Cramer, Johann Nepomuk Hummel, and Friedrich Kalkbrenner.[13] On the evidence of these musical sources, all of these embellishers – Ployer, Hoffmann, Cramer, Hummel, and Kalkbrenner – have two important things in common: they added many more notes than we are accustomed to hearing from even the most generous of today's ornamenters, and they wrote in styles quite different from Mozart's own. Largely for these very reasons (though also, in some instances, owing to their musical shortcomings), these embellishments have been widely condemned as "un-Mozartian" and anachronistic.[14]

The fundamental error of this way of thinking is the underlying assumption that the goal of embellishment is to make additions but still have the music sound as if every note had been written by Mozart. An alternative point of view, apparently shared by Ployer, Hoffmann, Cramer, Hummel, and Kalkbrenner, and more recently demonstrated by pianists like Wanda Landowska and Friedrich Gulda, is that embellishment was a way for performers to personalize the music – to put their own unabashedly un-Mozartian stamp on it.[15] The latter approach should not be misinterpreted as a sign of disregard for the Mozart style. Indeed, since the early nineteenth century, the challenge for performers – whether they liked it or not, or even whether they acknowledged it or not – has been to balance a sense of "Classical" style (whatever that may have meant at the time) with the perhaps conflicting desires to "speak" with a personal voice and satisfy contemporary standards of beauty and expressiveness. The difficulties that almost inevitably arise from this dilemma have surely contributed to the widespread retreat to the narrowly defined historical orientation described above: that "improvised" embellishments should sound as if Mozart had written them. Though obviously paradoxical, this view is nevertheless prevalent among pianists and scholars. As a result, much of the recent guidance regarding ornamentation has focused on examples from Mozart's own pen, not only the eight-bar decoration for K. 451, but other works that survive in both "plain" and embellished versions: the Adagio variation from the finale of the Piano Sonata in D major, K. 284/205b, the Adagio of the Piano Sonata in F major, K. 332/300k, the Adagio of the Piano Sonata in C minor, K. 457, and the soprano aria "Non sò d'onde viene," K. 294.[16] For the Piano Sonatas in D and in F, the "plain" readings derive from the autograph, while the embellished versions appeared in the first editions, presumably reflecting Mozart's aim to provide amateur pianists (the expected purchasers of the scores) with the kinds of ornaments that he might have improvised. For the aria and the C-minor Sonata, Mozart created the decorations expressly for particular performers within his orbit: respectively, his sister-in-law, the soprano Aloysia Weber, and his piano pupil Therese von Trattner, the sonata's dedicatee. Further examples of Mozart's ornamentation may be found in the embellished refrains in his Rondos for Piano in F major, K. 494, and in A minor, K. 511, and in the Adagio episodes in the finale of the Piano Concerto in C major, K. 415, though in these instances the ornaments are actually part of the musical conception.[17] Even with all of these models, modern pianists have tended to approach improvised embellishment with great caution. Rare indeed is the pianist willing, as was Mozart in bar 26 of the Adagio from the Sonata in F, K. 332/300k, to replace a thematic element with a long chromatic scale: precisely the kind of decorative substitution that some eminent musicologists have singled out for criticism in Ployer's embellishments for K. 488.[18]

Pianists willing to incorporate improvised embellishments into their performances can certainly learn a great deal from Mozart's own examples and from Robert Levin's suggestions, based as much on instinct and experience as on historical evidence, as to where it might be appropriate to add decorations: in slow movements, for (1) returns of the opening theme, (2) plain melodies with sparse, generally single-note accompaniments (what Levin calls "piano recitatives"), often found in the *B* sections of ternary or rondo forms, and (3) passages, often sequences, in which activity inexplicably relaxes; in fast movements, for (1) rondo refrains, (2) sequences involving literal motivic repetitions in longer note values, and (3) sustained notes that might benefit from a turn or trill to maintain momentum.[19] Levin's suggestions (and his accompanying examples) provide an excellent first step, one that too few pianists are willing to take. But those truly seeking to make their playing more beautiful and personal should feel emboldened to treat this knowledge not as a straitjacket but as a springboard. Historically "authentic" performance is, after all, a chimera. As Gustav Leonhardt wisely commented, "If one is convincing, what is offered will leave an authentic impression. If one strives to be authentic, it will never be convincing."[20]

Cadenzas and lead-ins (*Eingänge*)

Mozart's ability to improvise was legendary, and one therefore imagines that he could and did improvise cadenzas and lead-ins for his own piano concertos. However, the survival of his cadenzas and lead-ins for all but six of his original piano concertos suggests that he generally composed them in advance, rather than rely on the inspiration of the moment. Since the bulk of the extant cadenza manuscripts were part of the Mozart estate, Christoph Wolff has speculated that an entire portfolio of manuscripts, containing the cadenzas for K. 466, K. 467, K. 482, K. 491, K. 503, and K. 537, may also have been in the family collection but has been lost.[21] We know from a letter of 8 April 1785 to his sister that Mozart composed cadenzas for K. 466 and K. 467, but these have never been located. (K. 488 is the anomaly in this sequence: its relatively simple and largely nonthematic first-movement cadenza is written directly into the autograph score and may have been intended for amateur pianists,[22] leaving open the possibility that Mozart also wrote another, more ambitious one for his own use.) The survival of alternative cadenzas for some concertos indicates that he sometimes replaced or revised his cadenzas for particular occasions, either updating them, "improving" them, or perhaps simply providing something new to individualize those performances. He willingly shared his cadenzas with his sister and may even have written some specifically tailored to her skills and personality, as seems to have been the case with the *Eingänge* for the Finale of K. 271: those he sent to Nannerl in February 1783 (NMA: set C) are more prosaic and easier to play than the ones he devised for his own use, apparently the following month (NMA: set B).[23] Similarly, when he wrote to her on 21 July 1784, saying, "I would gladly have sent you the cadenzas for the other concertos, but you have no idea how much I have to do," he was explaining that he had no time to compose cadenzas specifically for her, since clearly he could have copied out, in less time than it took him to write the letter, the cadenzas that he himself had played.[24] Aside from his sister, he generally shared his cadenzas with no one (the prime exceptions being the concertos for two and three pianos, K. 365/316a and K. 242, in which other performers were necessarily involved). Another letter, written to his father on 22 January 1783, is often cited as evidence that Mozart usually improvised cadenzas rather than write them out beforehand: "I shall send the cadenzas [for K. 175/382] and lead-ins [for K. 271] to my dear sister at the first opportunity. I have not yet altered the lead-ins in the rondo, for whenever I play this concerto [K. 271], I always play whatever occurs to me at the moment."[25] Two points should be noted, however. First, Mozart mentions improvisation in connection not with the cadenzas, but with the shorter, often nonthematic lead-ins; secondly, his use of the word "altered" presupposes that he had previously composed lead-ins for the movement. When Mozart published his piano concertos he did not include cadenzas and lead-ins; purchasers were thus required to supply their own. From this evidence, it seems that Mozart considered his cadenzas not part of the work but part of his performance, and that when others played his concertos he would have expected to hear not his cadenzas but their own.[26] Indeed, while he was alive he did everything he could to *prevent* others from playing his cadenzas, yet that is precisely what most modern performers do.

Ferruccio Busoni offered a perspective on the cadenza and practical advice to performers in a preface to his edition of Beethoven's cadenzas (Hinrichshofen, 1901): "Pianists . . . who do not play their own cadenzas, should give preference to those composed by the Master. Cadenzas written by the performer are doubtless admissable as they are in unity and keeping with the performer's individuality; and this is evidently the composer's object in ceding his place to the performer. Whereas cadenzas emanating from third persons should be discarded, as introducing into the performance a third element still more alien to the whole." These same principles might be applied to the Mozart concertos, except that non-composing performers do not always have the option of a Mozart cadenza and so must resort to those written by "third persons." Almost all pianists these days play Mozart's cadenzas and lead-ins when they are extant, and when they are not, compose their own – but in Mozart's style. Alternatively, they adopt the most "Mozartian" ones available. (The problem, of course, is that our sense of what is "Mozartian" keeps changing, preventing a definitive solution.) This position is essentially the one recommended by the Badura-Skodas in their influential *Interpreting Mozart on the Keyboard*. It represents an aspiration, obviously impossible to realize, to play the concertos as Mozart himself might have played them and not, as we have seen, as he would have wanted and expected others to play them. To that end, the Badura-Skodas analyzed Mozart's extant cadenzas and lead-ins and proposed schemas, based on his *usual* practice, to serve as models for Mozart-style cadenza and lead-in composition.[27] In their desire to create cadenzas that could pass for "real" Mozart, they even recommend the forger's technique of copying passages from authentic cadenzas, transposing them if necessary. The pianist–musicologist Robert Levin has recently established a reputation for his ability to improvise convincingly Mozartian cadenzas, a skill demonstrated in his ongoing recorded cycle of the Mozart piano concertos on the L'Oiseau-Lyre (Decca) label, with Christopher Hogwood and the Academy of Ancient Music. In his ambition to re-create Mozart's own performances, he is philosophically close to the Badura-Skodas, although he has mastered and internalized certain features of Mozart's style to such an extent that he is able to improvise in concert what Paul Badura-Skoda had to work out on paper. (An audience, of course, will not know the difference unless it is told. Mozart's wasn't.) Levin also parts company with the Badura-Skodas in having the courage to improvise cadenzas even when Mozart's own are extant. On this point he agrees with Busoni, although the "individuality" which he projects is constrained by his ambition to improvise in the style of the music that Mozart composed. Ultimately and paradoxically Levin's improvisations are thus grounded in the same textual reverence that he seeks to defy. As a result, interest inevitably focuses more on the theatrics of the "act" of performance than on the music he improvises or how he plays it. In principle, though, Levin approaches Tovey's ideal: "an actual extemporization by a player capable of using the composer's language and above the temptation to display anything so banal as 'a review of the progress of music since the composer's date.'"[28]

Basso continuo[29]

A variety of evidence suggests that Mozart intended and expected the piano soloist to provide basso continuo accompaniment during the orchestral ritornellos and perhaps also during the shorter tutti passages within solo sections. The very layout of the autographs suggests as much. Unlike modern scores, which print the piano part in the middle of each system, above the strings and below the winds, brass, and timpani, Mozart placed it at the bottom of the page, directly above the cellos and double basses.[30] Moreover, by writing "CoB" (an abbreviation for *col basso*, meaning "with the [cello and double] bass [parts]") in the piano's lower stave during tutti passages, he was evidently directing the copyist or publisher to reproduce the bass line as the left hand of the solo part, and thereby to indicate that the piano was to double the bass. The addition of figures above this bass line, which was common in eighteenth-century manuscript and printed copies of the solo parts (notably, the editions of K. 413–15 published by Artaria in 1785), seems to confirm that the pianist was also expected to supply a chordal accompaniment above the bass. The composer himself provided figures in the autograph score of the Concerto for Three Pianos, K. 242 (Piano III only), while his father added them to the autographs of some of the other early concertos as well as to Nannerl's manuscript copies of the solo parts of nine of the concertos, including K. 466 and 467. There is also a manuscript solo part for the Piano Concerto in C, K. 246, written by a copyist but with a realization of the continuo in Mozart's handwriting.[31]

Musical evidence also seems to support the use of continuo. The Badura-Skodas identified some "thinly scored passages" in the tuttis that they felt benefited from adding continuo, and Ellwood Derr pointed to places where continuo playing seems necessary to provide musical continuity.[32] He cited, for example, the closing bars of the final movements of both K. 466 and K. 467, where the solo passagework halts on a dominant chord (in the former case, over a tonic pedal), ostensibly leaving it to the orchestra to complete the cadence. It makes better musical sense, Derr argued, for the pianist to join the orchestra in providing the necessary harmonic resolution. Also, from the point of view of musical theater it is dramatically disappointing for the soloist to approach the final cadence with much ado but lapse into silence during the climactic concluding gesture. This is more obvious in the concert hall than in recordings, since the visual element makes the listener more aware of who is *not* playing, especially if that individual is the soloist. Thus pianists with a sense of the theatrical, even if they renounce basso continuo elsewhere, instinctively play along with the orchestra during these concluding bars, especially in concert, where, for the sake of the audience if not of the music, they have a desire to appear active until the end (i.e., the applause). Since the piano will be largely covered by the orchestra, the effect is primarily visual anyway. Such factors associated with the "live" event – the visual drama, the relative inaudibility of the unwritten additions, and the evanescence of the moment – often liberate pianists from their ingrained sense of responsibility to the printed score and allow them, in this limited context, to indulge in a few bars of continuo playing. In recordings, on the other hand, the scales tip in the opposite direction: the permanence and repeatability of the recording; the presence of the all-hearing, analytical microphone controlled by a knob-twisting producer; the invisibility of the performers; and the replacement of the responsive, collective audience with the solitary, undemonstrative home listener (who "owns," rather than receives, the performance) all permit pianists who are not committed to adding basso continuo to refrain from providing it even at the concerto's close. Applause is not at risk, and they earn immunity from charges of cheap showmanship. As for the fortepianist inclined to play continuo, the medium of recording provides an added inducement by eliminating the balance problem.

For Charles Rosen, the practice of basso continuo (after ca. 1775) is inconsistent with the most essential, even the defining, feature of Classical concerto form – that it hinges on the drama of the solo entries, as opposed to the Baroque concerto, in which the most dramatic effects are produced by the re-entrance of the full orchestra after solo sections.[33] In Rosen's view, then, having the soloist provide basso continuo in the Classical piano concerto and thus play continuously throughout the work was an anachronism that undermined the dramatic effectiveness of the solo entrances and, by extension, the effect of the form itself. Therefore, to defend his analytical perspective, he needed to challenge the evidence supporting basso continuo. He flatly dismissed the musical arguments that basso continuo was sometimes necessary and suggested that the *col basso* instruction was merely to provide the soloist with cues.[34] Scrutinizing the 1785 Artaria edition of K. 415, he found serious errors in the figured bass, proving that it could not have been by Mozart. The discreet continuo part that Mozart supplied for K. 246 doubles the winds during their only solo, suggesting that it was intended exclusively for a performance without winds or perhaps even a chamber setting with solo strings (or, as Faye Ferguson has conjectured, for a two–piano performance, with a pupil playing the solo and the composer "improvising" an orchestral reduction on a second piano.[35])

Other scholars, notably the Badura-Skodas and Frederick Neumann, have taken Mozart's continuo realization for K. 246 at face value as indicative of what he would actually have played in his own concerto performances.[36] Pursuant to this hypothesis, a few principles might be inferred. The style of the realization is generally simple and chordal, in three- or four-part harmony, except in unison passages, when the pianist plays in octaves (*all'unisono*). The chordal realization occasionally doubles the main orchestral melody, but it never introduces independent thematic or motivic materials. At certain points the soloist refrains from adding chords and plays only the bass (*tasto solo*): throughout solo sections and sometimes even in the ritornellos, generally when the dynamic marking is *piano* (and the sound of the continuo could become obtrusive) and often at section ends. The ensuing solo entrances are thus set off, dramatized, and given sonic freshness by having the pianist in effect abandon the continuo function in the immediately preceding bars.[37]

Christoph Wolff, in his preface to the *Neue Mozart Ausgabe* edition (V/15/2, p. XIII), has suggested that Mozart wrote the realization for K. 246 not for his own use but for an amateur pianist, and that it was therefore simpler in style than what he himself would have improvised. Robert Levin reached a similar conclusion, noting that Mozart used K. 246 as a "teaching piece." Levin therefore recommends a more flexible and expressive approach to continuo playing, one that allows the pianist a broad range of options – not just chords, but melodic lines, combinations of melodies and chords, or even silence. The continuo, in Levin's view, need not be restricted to fulfilling its obligatory harmonic function, but might animate the proceedings by introducing independent melodic elements or rhythmic impulses. To illustrate these principles, Levin offers three different realizations for a brief passage from the Piano Concerto in C, K. 467 (first movement, bars 28–32).[38] In the second of these, the piano imitates in bar 29 the horn–trumpet motive of bar 28; in his third proposed realization, bars 30–1 quote a striking figure from an earlier C-major piano concerto, K. 415 (first movement, bars 70–1). Whether such ingenuity delights or distracts is a matter of personal taste.

A sampling of some prominent "period instrument" recordings of Mozart concertos reveals continuo playing that is often discreet to the point of being inaudible or indiscernible, especially in the more richly scored concertos. Ultimately, this may be a compliment to the recording teams for simulating an impression of concert-hall balance, which is typically even less favorable to the soloist. While individual instruments obviously differ, the fortepiano is really quite soft in relation to the ensemble, even when period orchestral instruments are used. Continuo playing on the fortepiano tends to be most apparent during quiet passages, which is paradoxically where the example of Mozart's own realization for K. 246 suggests that the soloist should probably play *tasto solo*. Frederick Neumann believed that continuo playing was inappropriate for performances on the modern piano because, in comparison with the fortepiano, its tone blends less well with the orchestra.[39] After all, as Neal Zaslaw has pointed out, the purpose of the continuo was not to provide a substantial sonic contribution, but to add "an almost subliminal ictus generally characteristic of orchestral sound of the period" while helping the orchestra keep together (particularly when the soloist was also directing from the keyboard).[40] A sonic impact that was only "subliminal" might be palatable even to Charles Rosen, who conceded (with heavy irony) that "from the point of view of modern performance, it would be acceptable if the pianist played the figured bass provided that no one could hear him."[41] Levin has argued that Mozart's concept of the concerto required continuo playing in order to "establish the *presence* of the soloist within the orchestra from the outset of the work."[42] Period instruments may thus offer a way for the opposing views of Rosen and Levin to be reconciled: the continuo-playing fortepianist can provide a "presence" without being heard.

In Peter Shaffer's *Amadeus*, the Emperor Joseph II criticizes *Die Ent-führung* for containing "too many notes," and the composer replies, "There are just as many notes, Majesty, neither more nor less, as are required." When this familiar anecdote was first reported, in 1804 by Jean-Baptiste-Antoine Suard, it was to preface the observation that Mozart "was later less content with his work; he made many corrections and cuts in it."[43] Shaffer, however, takes the exchange at face value, reflecting the prevailing modern view that Mozart's music is perfection itself. This opinion is memorably articulated by Salieri in the climactic scene ending Shaffer's first act, when he comments that Mozart's music "is finished as most music is never finished. Displace one note and there would be diminishment. Displace one phrase and the structure would fall." It requires some adjustment for listeners who share this view to become reconciled to the suggestion that Mozart's piano concertos might benefit from improvised embellishment or basso continuo, partic-ularly when they have become accustomed to hearing the works without such additions. From their perspective, embellishment is easier to accept if it imitates Mozart's idiom or, better yet, borrows figures or formulas from his compositions, and basso continuo is more palatable if the pianist participates but introduces nothing of substance.

Pedal piano[44]

The handbill announcing Mozart's première of K. 467 noted that "he not only will play a *new*, just *finished fortepiano concerto*, but will also use an especially *large pedal fortepiano* in *improvising*." This "large pedal fortepiano" was almost certainly a self-contained instrument, consisting of its own pedal-operated "keyboard," action, strings, soundboard, and case, which rested on the floor beneath a fortepiano and was played in conjunction with it using the feet, like the pedalboard of an organ. Leopold Mozart described the mechanism in a letter to his daughter, written on 12 March 1785, two days after the concert: "[Wolfgang] has had a large fortepiano pedal made, which stands under the instrument and is about two feet longer [than the fortepiano] and extremely heavy. It is taken to the Mehlgrube [where he was offering a series of six subscrip-tion concerts] every Friday and has also been taken to Count Zichy's and to Prince Kaunitz's."[45] Other documents describe Mozart improvising and performing improvisatory-style compositions on the pedal piano. A visitor to the composer's lodgings on 24 August 1788 noted that "the master twice *extemporized* on a *pedal pianoforte*, so wonderfully! so wonderfully! that I quite lost myself," while his companion commented that Mozart "played free improvisations for us in such a manner that I wished that I could improvise like this; his pedal in the second improvisation in particular made the most agreeable impression."[46] Joseph Frank, an amateur composer and pianist, recalled hearing Mozart play one of his fantasias, presumably the Fantasia in C minor, K. 475: "The piano became a completely different instrument under his fingers. He had had it amplified by means of a second keyboard, which he used as a pedal."[47] Thomas Attwood, Mozart's English pupil, recalled the composer's motivation for acquiring the pedal piano and seems to imply that he used it on a particular occasion relevant to the present discussion: "He was so fond of Sebastian Bach's Preludes & Fugues that he had a separate Pianoforte with Pedals, fixed under the Other – was very kind to all of Talent who came to Vienna & generally played at their Benefit Concerts with the Pianofortes as directed above – The last time I heard him [23 February 1787], He play'd his concerto in D Minor [K. 466] & 'Non temere' [K. 505] at [Ann] Storace's Benefit for whom he composed that Cantata with the Pianoforte solo . . ."[48]

We thus know that Mozart acquired a pedal piano around 1785 and still possessed it at the time of his death, when it was included in the inventory of his possessions.[49] He used it frequently in concerts (at least in February–March 1785 and apparently in February 1787) and both improvised and played improvisatory-style compositions on it. Though proof is lacking, circumstantial evidence makes it tempting to speculate that he might also have used it when he played his piano concertos, particularly K. 466 and K. 467. The mechanism was literally beneath his feet on 10 March 1785, when he played K. 467, and the urge to make use of it to reinforce the bass must have been very strong indeed. With rather less certainty, the pedal piano may also be linked to two separate performances of K. 466. The première was given at the Mehlgrube on 11 February 1785, the very day that Leopold Mozart arrived in Vienna, and although his report of the concert made no mention of the pedal piano, he later commented that the instrument was taken to the Mehlgrube "every Friday" for the series of six weekly subscription concerts.

Example 5 K. 466/I, autograph reading

Leopold described the program as having included symphonies and two arias, but no composition other than the concerto that would have required a piano. Therefore, if the pedal piano was used on this occasion it would probably have been for K. 466. Attwood's testimony regarding the performance on 23 February 1787 is even less conclusive. He noted that Mozart "generally played" at the benefit concerts of others using the pedal piano, and in the next breath he recalled hearing him play K. 466 and a concert aria at Ann Storace's benefit concert.

The most intriguing evidence pointing to the possible use of the pedal piano in K. 466 is in the autograph itself. In the first movement, from bar 88 to the first beat of bar 90, Mozart's first draft had running sixteenth notes for the right hand and single bass notes for the left, doubling the timpani at the unison in bars 88–9 and an octave lower on the first beat of bar 90. He then revised the passage, moving the bass notes down an octave in bars 88–9 and adding a series of mid-range chords (see Example 5). To play all of these notes would require three hands – or a pedal piano. Robert Levin, however, considers it "implausible for Mozart to have conceived a work exclusively for his own use on a pedal piano, yet call for it in only 2½ measures."[50] He therefore speculates that Mozart intended, but neglected, to cross out the low bass notes when he added the mid-range chords.

David Rowland draws the opposite conclusion from the autograph, arguing that Mozart's habit in his concerto autographs of notating the solo part immediately above the cello–bass line made it easy for him to double that line with the pedals whenever he so desired.[51] For example, the theme at bars 147–54, 310–17 and 363–70 of the finale would clearly benefit from such an added pedal part, as the harmonies in the piano left hand are incomplete without the accompanying cellos and basses. In bars 88–90 of the first movement, on the other hand, the strings are silent and the piano is accompanied only by the winds and brass, which might have motivated the composer to write out the pedal part for these bars. Significantly, too, this passage occurs relatively early in the score, in the first solo statement, after which time pressures might have convinced him to leave out the part for the pedalboard and instead rely on the adjacent cello–bass stave and his skill at improvisation. Rowland supports his argument in favor of the pedal piano by citing his personal experience of performing K. 467 on that instrument. Using the pedals, he claims, not only "adds to the projection of the sound that can otherwise have difficulty in carrying over the orchestra," but "also adds attack and definition to the bass line, and substance to the orchestral tuttis." The last comment presumably refers to the soloist's continuo playing.

Orchestra size and seating

A historically based discussion of orchestra size and seating arrangement must begin by recognizing the variety of settings in which Mozart's piano concertos were performed during his lifetime. Since relatively few halls in the eighteenth century were built expressly for presenting concerts, places originally designed for other purposes were most commonly used. Setting aside the option of outdoor concerts and pointing out that concerto performances in churches would have featured solo violin, trumpet, or organ, rather than harpsichord or piano, Neal Zaslaw has identified three settings in which piano concertos were performed: the salon (a room intended for social gatherings of various kinds in a middle-class or aristocratic home), the hall (a large room with a high ceiling, such as might be found in "palaces, stately homes, colleges, monasteries, taverns, and the like"), and the theater.[52]

Iconographic evidence indicates that for concerto performances in salons, the fortepiano would have been placed broadside, with the orchestral instruments – typically only one player per part – behind it in a single row. This "chamber" arrangement might have worked well for Mozart's earlier concertos, but not for the later, more richly scored ones with obbligato winds, especially since a full complement of wind players, in all probability, would rarely have been on hand for such modest home concerts. This was the situation at Leopold Mozart's house, as Wolfgang reminded him when he sent copies of the Piano Concertos, K. 449–451

111

and 453: "I formed the opinion, which I still hold, that the music would not be of much use to you, because except for the E♭ concerto [K. 449], which can be performed a quattro without wind-instruments, the other three concertos all have wind-instrument accompaniment; and you very rarely have wind-instrument players at your house."[53] Mozart surely had such home performances in mind when, hoping to sell subscriptions for manuscript copies of the Piano Concertos, K. 413–415, he advertised in the *Wiener Zeitung* (15 January 1783) that the works "may be performed either with a large orchestra with wind instruments or merely *a quattro*, viz. with 2 violins, 1 viola and violoncello."[54] Obviously, the piano concertos with obbligato winds (like K. 466 and 467) were not susceptible to this sort of reduction. Consequently a market developed in the early nineteenth century for arrangements of such concertos, either for piano solo or for a chamber ensemble consisting of piano, flute, violin, and cello. Such arrangements were intended either for home use or for public "concert" performances in small towns that could not support a full orchestra.

The première of the Piano Concerto in D minor, K. 466, took place in the second category of concerto venue: a "hall," specifically, a large room on the second floor of the Mehlgrube, a city-owned building constructed in 1697 and located on the Neuer Markt.[55] A restaurant occupied the ground floor, and the large room on the floor above was used not only for concerts, but also for banquets and balls. In smaller adjoining rooms food and beverages were served, and gaming tables were available.[56] According to Leopold Mozart's reports, there were more than 150 subscribers, including "a great many members of the aristocracy," to the concert series that Mozart presented at the Mehlgrube between 11 February and 18 March 1785.[57] Since Leopold seemed so pleased with the attendance, we might estimate a seating capacity for the hall of around 150–200. However, for a concert presented at the Mehlgrube by the Gesellschaft der Musikfreunde on 12 November 1807, 1309 tickets were distributed. It must have been extremely crowded, with many forced to stand or be consigned to the adjoining rooms, since the organizers moved all subsequent programs that season to a larger hall at the university.[58]

Iconographic evidence suggests that in "halls" like the Mehlgrube the players would probably have occupied a low platform situated not at the end of the room, but against one of the long walls.[59] The seating plan for K. 466 would probably have been similar to the one recommended in 1802 by the piano-maker and Mozart pupil Nannette Stein Streicher:

> In performing concertos, especially Mozart's, one should move the fortepiano several feet nearer [the audience] than the orchestra is. Directly behind the piano leave just the violins. The bass-line and wind instruments should be further back, the latter more than the former.[60]

For concerts like Mozart's, for which the featured artist actually hired the orchestra, it was usual to have only a single rehearsal, the morning of the performance.[61] For the première of K. 466, on 11 February 1785, there was not even time to read through the finale, since Mozart was busy supervising the copying of the parts. Leopold's report that "the orchestra played splendidly" is hard to believe, given the circumstances. (In contrast, when Leopold's seventeen-year-old pupil Heinrich Marchand rehearsed the concerto for a performance in Salzburg on 22 March 1786 it took three playings of the finale to get the orchestra to play together and keep up with the soloist.) Adalbert Gyrowetz, one of whose symphonies was programmed in Mozart's Mehlgrube series, noted in his presumed autobiography that Mozart had hired a "full theater orchestra" for these concerts.[62] This was most likely the orchestra of the Burgtheater, where, four days later, on 15 February 1785, Mozart again played the D-minor Piano Concerto, in a concert given by the singer Elisabeth Distler.

The Burgtheater, representing the third category of concert venue, was also the site of the première of the Piano Concerto in C, K. 467, less than a month later, on 10 March 1785. Located on the Michaelerplatz, the Burgtheater was built in 1741 and renovated numerous times before its closing in 1888. Plans reflecting the state of the building during the 1780s show an oval-shaped house, with seating on the floor divided into two sections, ostensibly according to the social rank of the spectators: the Noble Parquet in front, and behind it the slightly elevated Second Parquet, with rows of benches and standing room at the rear.[63] (Social segregation was not complete, however, as individuals connected to the theater, including composers and performers, could obtain passes granting admission to the Noble Parquet.[64]) Four balconies surrounded the floor. The lower two held the boxes rented on an annual basis by the nobility, plus, in the first tier, one box overlooking the stage, reserved for the director, and three "Imperial loges" (one in the center and two on the right) overlooking the orchestra, which occupied the floor at the front of the stage. The upper two balconies were galleries with benches and standing room. When jam-packed, the Burgtheater may have accommodated as many as 1800 spectators, but most estimates of the audience capacity are much lower, ranging from around 1000 to 1350.[65]

According to a Vienna theater almanac of 1782, the Burgtheater orchestra comprised 35 players: six first and six second violins, four violas, three cellos, three basses, pairs of flutes, oboes, clarinets, bassoons, horns, and trumpets, and one timpanist.[66] (This is precisely the size and composition of the London Classical Players in the Melvyn Tan/Roger Norrington EMI recordings of K. 466, 488, 491, and 503.) Assuming that these figures are also reliable for 1785, that the full theater orchestra participated in Mozart's concerts in both the Burgtheater and the Mehlgrube, and that the entire ensemble was used for the concerto accompaniments, we can conclude that the orchestra for the first performances of K. 466 and 467 consisted of around 32 players (one of the flutes and the two clarinets not being needed).

It is unfortunate that the manuscript orchestral parts that Mozart used for his Viennese performances have apparently not survived, for these might have revealed the number of players for each string part. However, manuscript parts for K. 466, currently in the archive of St. Peter's in Salzburg, seem to be the ones that Leopold Mozart had copied in Salzburg for Marchand's 1786 performance.[67] While they cannot, therefore, be associated with Wolfgang's Vienna performances, they are perhaps the next best thing. The Salzburg materials consist of two first and two second violin parts, one part for both first and second violas, a cello part that also included the double bass line, a separate bass part, and single parts for the remaining instruments. Assuming that two players read from each of the string parts, which is not a certainty, there would have been at most 14 strings in the Salzburg orchestra – eight violins, two violas, one cello, and three double basses (as opposed to 22 strings at the Burgtheater) – provided, of course, that these surviving parts represent the entire set and that no duplicates have been lost or discarded. The two "extra" violin parts, after all, are not really duplicates but *ripieno* parts, which call upon the additional violinists to play during the tuttis but which mark rests during the solos, when the orchestra is essentially accompanying. These *ripieno* parts support the theory that the "solo" and "tutti" indications marked in some of the orchestral parts and autograph scores for Mozart's concertos are actually cues for this *ripieno* practice and not merely structural signposts.[68] Some contemporary theorists corroborate this convention, including Heinrich Christoph Koch in the definition of "tutti" in his *Musikalisches Lexikon* (1802).[69]

The Salzburg parts for K. 466 demonstrate that the copyist (or Leopold Mozart, directing him) had been able to designate the solo and tutti divisions even when they were not explicitly marked in the score, suggesting that the practice may have been more widespread than the autograph scores themselves might indicate. On the other hand, Dexter Edge, who examined nearly five hundred sets of manuscript orchestral parts for eighteenth-century Viennese concertos, found that only about five percent of them included *ripieno* parts. Indeed, the vast majority of these sets (84%) had only single copies of each part, leading Edge to conclude cautiously that "eighteenth-century Viennese concertos were sometimes performed with single players on a part."[70]

In the first movement of K. 466, the Salzburg *ripieno* parts direct the full complement of strings (whatever their actual numbers may have been) to play in the opening ritornello (bars 1–77); the brief tutti passage in the solo exposition that articulates the half-cadence on the dominant (bars 112–14); the ritornello following the solo exposition (bars 174–92); the beginning of the recapitulation, as far as the tutti half-cadence on the dominant (bars 254–87); and the ritornellos preceding and following the cadenza (bars 356–97). The only problematic part of this scheme is the treatment of the beginning of the recapitulation. The difficulty arises because, on the one hand, this section starts with the orchestra alone and tends to follow the thematic order of the ritornello (factors which would suggest full strings), but, on the other hand, the solo joins in for two stretches (which would seem to call for reduced strings). The solution chosen in Salzburg presumably worked because the consistent use of full strings appropriately reflected the continuity of the orchestral contribution (in bars 254–80), but without seriously threatening to cover the soloist: in bars 261–8 the piano's vigorous broken-octave figuration lies an octave above and is rhythmically more active than the first violin part, which it doubles much of the time, and in bars 278–80 the piano's triplet arpeggios rise above and are rhythmically distinct from the orchestra, which is marked *piano*.

In the Romanze, the Salzburg parts call for the full strings to play in each presentation of the refrain (bars 9–39, 76–83, and 135–41), which is possible since the piano and orchestra play in alternation and never together. During the episodes and coda, however, the strings consistently accompany the piano and are consequently reduced. In the third movement, the *ripieno* parts join in for the opening ritornello (bars 13–62), the tutti leading to the development (bars 180–95), the tutti preceding the cadenza (bars 337–45), and the entire coda, with the single exception of bars 402–9, which involve the soloist and are marked *piano*. In all three movements, the *ripieno* practice thus helps to articulate the form, while serving a variety of practical and expressive functions, enumerated by Neal Zaslaw: "to enhance dynamic and timbral contrasts, to overcome the problem of insufficient rehearsal time, to minimize potential difficulties of balance between fortepiano and orchestra, and perhaps also to create more flexible accompaniments."[71]

Richard Maunder has speculated that, when Mozart performed his piano concertos in the theater, the orchestra may have been in the pit, while he alone occupied the stage.[72] Putting the soloist in this privileged position, Maunder reasoned, would have helped solve potential balance problems between the fortepiano and the orchestra, whose players would have been seated facing the stage, with their backs to the audience. Such a "theatrical staging" of the concerto moreover made manifest the genre's affinity with the operatic aria. Daniel Heartz, however, has offered evidence that it was customary for Lenten concert and oratorio performances at the Burgtheater to follow the Italian practice and have all of the musicians on stage: the orchestra, soloists, and chorus.[73] He speculated, though, that the arrangement described by Maunder might have been a practical necessity at other times of year, when theater rehearsals and stage sets might have made it difficult to rearrange the stage for an orchestra. Mary Sue Morrow has challenged this reasoning, arguing that rehearsals were often held elsewhere and that the theater's repertory system would have required that the sets be struck after each performance anyway.[74] Maunder's theory seems unlikely from a purely logistical point of view, given the mixed nature of Mozart's typical concert programs. For example, his concert of 23 March 1783 at the

Burgtheater began and ended with movements of the "Haffner" Symphony, with arias, concertos, concertante movements, and solo piano works interspersed in between. It would have seemed odd for the orchestra to start the program on stage, then repair to the pit, only to re-ascend at the end of the concert for the "Haffner" finale. Even odder would have been for the orchestra to remain in the pit throughout, leaving the audience to face an empty stage at the start and conclusion of the evening. For performances of Mozart's concertos in the theater, then, we may imagine all of the performers on stage, arranged according to the seating plan recommended above by Nannette Stein Streicher.

Notes

1 Introduction

1 Charles Rosen, *The Classical Style*, expanded edn. (New York: Norton, 1997), p. 228.

2 Donald Francis Tovey, *Essays in Musical Analysis* (London: Oxford University Press, 1935–44), vol. 6, *Supplementary Essays, Glossary and Index* (1939), p. 141.

3 Mendelssohn's cadenzas, originally written for an 1832 performance, are not extant, although he wrote out some portions of the end of the first-movement cadenza in a letter to his sister, following a subsequent performance in 1836. Clara Schumann, who heard him play it in 1841, noted that he "ended especially the last movement with a very beautifully artful cadenza." See R. Larry Todd, "Mozart According to Mendelssohn: A Contribution to *Rezeptionsgeschichte*," in *Perspectives on Mozart Performance*, ed. R. Larry Todd and Peter Williams (Cambridge: Cambridge University Press, 1991), pp. 176–7 and 190–3; and *The Marriage Diaries of Robert & Clara Schumann: From Their Wedding Day through the Russia Trip*, ed. Gerd Nauhaus, trans. Peter Ostwald (Boston: Northeastern University Press, 1993), pp. 57–8.

4 *Letters of Clara Schumann and Johannes Brahms: 1853–1896*, ed. Berthold Litzman (New York: Longmans, Green and Co., 1927), II:34.

5 On Mozart's contrasting paired compositions, see A. Hyatt King, *Mozart in Retrospect: Studies in Criticism and Bibliography* (London: Oxford University Press, 1955), pp. 180–7. As Hyatt King points out, the Piano Concertos in A major, K. 488, and C minor, K. 491, were both entered in Mozart's personal thematic catalogue in March 1786. However, the impulse to regard them as such a pair must be tempered by the knowledge that the former was apparently begun much earlier, in 1783–4 or 1784–5. On the dating of the autograph of K. 488, see Alan Tyson, *Mozart: Studies of Autograph Scores* (Cambridge, Mass.: Harvard University Press, 1987), pp. 152–3.

6 On Mozart's mental and physical health, particularly the possibility that he suffered from cyclothymic disorder, a bipolar condition which causes a pre-

disposition to manic-depression, see Peter J. Davies, *Mozart in Person: His Character and Health* (Westport, Conn.: Greenwood Press, 1989), and "Mozart's Manic-Depressive Tendencies," *Musical Times* 128 (1987): 123–6 and 191–6.

7 *The Letters of Mozart and His Family*, ed. and trans. Emily Anderson, 3rd edn. (New York and London: W. W. Norton, 1985), no. 555, p. 917.

8 Martin Chusid, "The Significance of D Minor in Mozart's Dramatic Music," *Mozart-Jahrbuch 1965/66*, p. 89. On Mozart's use of minor keys see also Wilhelm Fischer, "Zu W. A. Mozarts Tonartenwahl und Harmonik," *Mozart-Jahrbuch 1952*, pp. 9–16. K. 466 is discussed in relation to eighteenth-century theories of key characteristics and affect and in the context of a "tradition" of D-minor keyboard concertos (encompassing works by J. S. Bach, C. P. E. Bach, J. C. Bach, Johann Gottlieb Goldberg, Johann Gottfried Müthel) in Lothar Hoffmann-Erbrecht, "Klavierkonzert und Affektgestaltung: Bemerkungen zu einigen d-Moll-Klavierkonzerten des 18. Jahrhunderts," *Deutsches Jahrbuch der Musikwissenschaft für 1971*, ed. Rudolf Eller (Leipzig: Peters, 1973), pp. 86–110.

9 Stuart Feder, "Mozart in D Minor – or, The Father's Blessing; The Father's Curse," in *The Pleasures and Perils of Genius: Mostly Mozart*, ed. Peter Ostwald and Leonard S. Zegans (Madison, Conn.: International Universities Press, 1993), p. 117–31.

10 See Rita Steblin, *A History of Key Characteristics in the Eighteenth and Early Nineteenth Centuries* (1983; reprint edn., Rochester, N.Y.: University of Rochester Press, 1996).

11 Elaine Sisman, in her discussion of Mozart's key choices for his last three symphonies, stresses the "grandiose, military, majestic" character ascribed by theorists to C major and thus connects the "Jupiter" Symphony with Austria's ongoing war with the Turks; *Mozart: The 'Jupiter' Symphony* (Cambridge: Cambridge University Press, 1993), pp. 26–7. See also her discussion of the "learned style" "as a signifier of the sublime" in the "Jupiter" finale, pp. 68–79.

12 On Mozart's finances see William J. Baumol and Hilda Baumol, "On the Economics of Musical Composition in Mozart's Vienna," in *On Mozart*, ed. James M. Morris (Cambridge: Woodrow Wilson Center Press and Cambridge University Press, 1994), pp. 72–101; Julia Moore, "Mozart in the Market-Place," *Journal of the Royal Musical Association* 114 (1989): 18–42; and Moore, "Mozart Mythologized or Modernized?" *Journal of Musicological Research* 12 (1992): 83–109. On the financial aspects of concert presenting, see Mary Sue Morrow, *Concert Life in Haydn's Vienna: Aspects of a Developing Musical and Social Institution* (Stuyvesant, N.Y.: Pendragon

Press, 1989), pp. 109–39; for commentary on and correction of some relevant points, see also Dexter Edge's review of this book in *Haydn Yearbook* 17 (1992): 108–66.

13 Leopold's reports were contained in his letters to his daughter, extracts of which are reproduced in Anderson, ed., *The Letters of Mozart and His Family*, pp. 885–9.

14 Tovey, *Essays in Musical Analysis*, vol. 3, *Concertos* (1936), pp. 6–7.

15 Heinrich Christoph Koch, *Introductory Essay on Composition [1782–93]: The Mechanical Rules of Melody, Sections 3 and 4*, trans. Nancy Kovaleff Baker (New Haven and London: Yale University Press, 1983), p. 209.

16 Susan McClary, "A Musical Dialectic from the Enlightenment: Mozart's Piano Concerto in G Major, K. 453, Movement 2," *Cultural Critique* 4 (1986): 129–69.

17 Helen Shively, "Mozart and the Public Sphere: Toward a Hermeneutic Model for the Piano Concertos," unpublished typescript, 1995; and Jürgen Habermas, *The Structural Transformation of the Public Sphere: An Inquiry into a Category of Bourgeois Society*, trans. Thomas Burger (Cambridge, Mass.: MIT Press, 1989).

18 Joseph Kerman, "Mozart's Piano Concertos and Their Audience," in *Write All These Down: Essays on Music* (Berkeley: University of California Press, 1994), pp. 322–34. See also his "Mozart à la Mode," *New York Review of Books*, 18 May 1989, pp. 50–2.

19 Mozart's use of winds in his piano concertos is discussed in Irving R. Eisley, "Mozart's Concertato Orchestra," *Mozart-Jahrbuch 1876/77*, pp. 9–20: and Christoph Wolff, "Aspects of Instrumentation in Mozart's Orchestral Music," in *L'interprétation de la musique classique de Haydn à Schubert: Colloque international, Evry, 13–15 octobre 1977* (Paris: Fondation pour l'art & la recherche and Editions Minkoff, 1980), pp. 37–43.

20 H. C. Robbins Landon, "The Concertos: (2) Their Musical Origin and Development," in *The Mozart Companion*, ed. H. C. Robbins Landon and Donald Mitchell (London: Rockliff, 1956), pp. 234–82; Denis Forman, *Mozart's Concerto Form: The First Movements of the Piano Concertos* (New York: Praeger, 1971), pp. 27–46; Hoffmann-Erbrecht, "Klavierkonzert und Affektgestaltung"; John A. Meyer, "The Keyboard Concertos of Johann Christian Bach and Their Influence on Mozart," *Miscellanea Musicologica* 10 (1979): 59–73; Jane R. Stevens, "The Importance of C. P. E. Bach for Mozart's Piano Concertos," in *Mozart's Piano Concertos: Text, Context, Interpretation*, ed. Neal Zaslaw, (Ann Arbor: University of Michigan Press, 1996), pp. 211–36. Ellwood Derr argues that Mozart's piano concertos, including K. 467, contain "borrowings" from the music of other composers,

especially J. C. Bach, in "Some Thoughts on the Design of Mozart's Opus 4, the 'Subscription Concertos' (K. 414, 413, and 415)," in *Mozart's Piano Concertos: Text, Context, Interpretation*, ed. Zaslaw, pp. 187–210.

21 Jane R. Stevens, "An 18th-Century Description of Concerto First-Movement Form," *Journal of the American Musicological Society* 24 (1971): 85–95; Shelley Davis, "H. C. Koch, the Classic Concerto, and the Sonata-Form Retransition," *Journal of Musicology* 2 (1983): 45–61. A valuable critique of Koch is Nancy K. Baker, "The Aesthetic Theories of Heinrich Christoph Koch," *International Review of the Aesthetics and Sociology of Music* 8 (1977): 183–209.

22 See, for example, the essays concerned with "the interconnections between Mozart's piano concertos and eighteenth-century opera" in *Mozart's Piano Concertos: Text, Context, Interpretation*, ed. Zaslaw, pp. 75–186: viz., Wye Jamison Allanbrook, "Comic Issues in Mozart's Piano Concertos"; James Webster, "Are Mozart's Concertos 'Dramatic'? Concerto Ritornellos versus Aria Introductions in the 1780s"; Janet M. Levy, "Contexts and Experience: Problems and Issues"; and Martha Feldman, "Staging the Virtuoso: Ritornello Procedure in Mozart, from Aria to Concerto."

23 Edwin J. Simon, "The Double Exposition in the Classic Concerto," *Journal of the American Musicological Society* 10 (1957): 111–8.

24 Jane R. Stevens, "Theme, Harmony, and Texture in Classic–Romantic Descriptions of Concerto First-Movement Form," *Journal of the American Musicological Society* 27 (1974): 25–60. See also Scott L. Balthazar, "Intellectual History and Concepts of the Concerto: Some Parallels from 1750 to 1850," *Journal of the American Musicological Society* 36 (1983): 39–72.

25 See Leonard Ratner, "*Ars Combinatoria*: Chance and Choice in Eighteenth-Century Music," in *Studies in Eighteenth-Century Music: A Tribute to Karl Geiringer on his Seventieth Birthday*, ed. H. C. Robbins Landon and Roger E. Chapman (New York: Oxford University Press, 1970), pp. 343–63.

26 Mozart, *Anleitung zum Componiren von Walzern so viele man will vermittlest zweier Würfel ohne etwas von der Musik oder Composition zu verstehen* (Berlin: Simrock, 1793).

27 Formal studies in the Germanic tradition include: on first-movement form, Konrad Küster, *Formale Aspekte des ersten Allegros in Mozarts Konzerten* (Kassel: Bärenreiter, 1991), and Robert Forster, *Die Kopfsätze der Klavierkonzerte Mozarts und Beethovens. Gesamtaufbau, Solokadenz und Schlussbildung*, Studien zur Musik, no. 10 (Munich: Wilhelm Fink, 1992); on middle movements, Klaus Weising, *Die Sonatenform in den langsamen Konzertsätzen Mozarts* (Hamburg: Karl Dieter Wagner, 1970), and Marion Brück, *Die langsamen Sätze in Mozarts Klavierkonzerten. Untersuchungen zur Form*

und zum musikalischen Satz, Studien zur Musik, no. 12 (Munich: Wilhelm Fink, 1994); and on finales, Rudolf Bockholdt, "Auftritt, Wiederkehr und Beendigung. Rondo-Form und Konzert-Realität in den Schlusssätzen von Mozarts Klavierkonzerten," in *Mozart Studien*, vol. 1, ed. Manfred Hermann Schmid (Tutzing: Hans Schneider, 1992), pp. 43–58, and Thomas Schlage, "Bemerkungen zu den Finali der in Wien entstandenen Klavierkonzerte Wolfgang Amadeus Mozarts," *Archiv für Musikwissenschaft* 54 (1997): 228–42.

2 Twentieth-century theories of Mozart's concerto form

1 *Essays in Musical Analysis* (London: Oxford University Press, 1935–44), vol. 3, *Concertos* (1936), pp. 3–27. Tovey assigned the Baroque concertos (by Bach and Handel) to volume 2, the second of the "Symphonies" volumes, in a special category of "Orchestral Polyphony" that also included two of Bach's orchestral suites as well as various overtures, fugues, and concertos by Beethoven, Röntgen, Vaughan Williams, and Holst.

2 See Stevens, "Theme, Harmony, and Texture in Classic–Romantic Descriptions of Concerto First-Movement Form," pp. 56–7.

3 Mark Evan Bonds, *Wordless Rhetoric: Musical Form and the Metaphor of the Oration* (Cambridge, Mass., and London: Harvard University Press, 1991), p. 142.

4 One notes, for example, in his discussion of Mozart's concertos in *The Classical Style* such comments as "the drama . . . unfold[s] as if impelled from within" (p. 189), and "much of it is audibly derived from the opening phrase" (p. 199), while serial thinking informs the observation relative to K. 271 that Mozart initially uses only eleven of the chromatic notes, withholding the twelfth for a particular effect (p. 201).

5 Denis Forman offered essentially the same scheme as the typical North German concerto form, exemplified by C. P. E. Bach, though he did not identify the submediant as the likely harmonic goal of *S2*. See his *Mozart's Concerto Form: The First Movements of the Piano Concertos*, p. 36.

6 Using as an example Mozart's Piano Concerto in D, K. 107 No. 1 (his concerto arrangement of J. C. Bach's Piano Sonata, Op. 5 No. 2), Rosen notes that Mozart used a relatively heavy scoring in the orchestra to reinforce important harmonic arrivals within the sonata form: the half-cadence before the second group and the cadence at the end of the exposition, the cadence on the relative minor near the end of the development, the half-cadence shortly before the retransition that culminates in the first theme of the recapitulation, the cadence at the end of the first group in the recapitulation, the cadential six-four introducing the cadenza, and the closing ritornello.

7 In his *Who Wrote the Mozart Four-Wind Concertante?* (Stuyvesant, N.Y.: Pendragon Press, 1988), p. 60, Levin describes this survey as also having included C. P. E. Bach and Michael Haydn, and he notes that he subsequently extended the investigation to include works by "Bréval, Cambini, Devienne, etc."

8 This study was included in Levin's Harvard undergraduate thesis, "The Unfinished Works of W. A. Mozart" (1968), and was subsequently excerpted in his article "Das Konzert für Klavier und Violine D-dur KV Anh. 56/315f und das Klarinettenquintett B-dur KV Anh. 91/516c: Ein Ergänzungsversuch," *Mozart-Jahrbuch 1968/70*, pp. 304–26. Levin subsequently completed two other concerto fragments: the Sinfonia Concertante in A Major for Violin, Viola, Cello, and Orchestra, K. Anh. 104/320e, and the Oboe Concerto in F Major, K. 293/416f.

9 Arthur Hutchings, in *A Companion to Mozart's Piano Concertos*, 2nd edn. (London: Oxford University Press, 1950), also commented on the dynamic shifts of the opening ritornello. Indeed, in analyzing K. 466 as the "typical Mozart concerto" he defined the "five musical paragraphs" of the opening ritornello purely in terms of the *p-f-p-f-p* dynamic pattern (p. 6).

10 See Robert Winter, "The Bifocal Close and the Evolution of the Viennese Classical Style," *Journal of the American Musicological Society* 42 (1989): 275–337. In the opening ritornello of K. 413/387a the *forte* half-cadence is followed by a lyric "second" theme that begins in the dominant (as in a sonata exposition), but the theme does not sustain the new key and folds back to the tonic. In the solo exposition, the orchestra plays this lyric theme in the dominant, just as it had done in the ritornello, but at the point where it would veer into the tonic key (undesirable in an exposition) the piano enters to steer the theme back to the dominant. In other words, rather than *introduce* the lyric theme in the exposition, the piano *rescues* it. (In the recapitulation, when the orchestra plays the lyric theme in the tonic, it naturally heads toward the subdominant, and the piano must again intervene, this time to restore the tonic.) In K. 482 the recapitulation begins by following the thematic sequence of the opening ritornello (but with the participation of the piano) through the "second theme" in the tonic, thus reinterpreting the ritornello's refusal to modulate as the recapitulation's resolution.

11 Cuthbert M. Girdlestone, *Mozart's Piano Concertos*, 2nd edn. (London: Cassel, 1958), p. 26. Levin, "Das Konzert für Klavier und Violine," p. 310.

12 See Levin's comments about the "speculative character" and "experimental" aspects of this movement in "Mozart's Keyboard Concertos," in *Eighteenth-Century Keyboard Music*, ed. Robert L. Marshall (New York: Schirmer Books, 1994), pp. 363–5.

13 Robert D. Levin, "Improvisation and Musical Structure in the Mozart Con-

certi," in *L'interprétation de la musique classique de Haydn à Schubert: Colloque international, Evry, 13–15 octobre 1977* (Paris: Fondation pour l'art & la recherche and Editions Minkoff, 1980), p. 51.

14 *Ibid.*

15 Levin, "Das Konzert für Klavier und Violine," p. 312, citing Théodore de Wyzewa and Georges de Saint-Foix, *Wolfgang Amédée Mozart: sa vie musicale et son oeuvre*, 5 vols. (Paris, 1912–46), III: 67,147.

16 See Rosen, *Sonata Forms*, rev. edn. (New York: Norton, 1988), pp. 246–61.

17 Kerman, "Mozart's Piano Concertos and Their Audience," p. 326.

18 See Rosen, *Sonata Forms*, p. 83.

19 See the Piano Concertos K. 175, K. 238, K. 242, K. 246, K. 365/316a, K. 414/385p, K. 449, K. 450, K. 453, K. 466, K. 467, K. 482, K. 488, K. 491, K. 503, K. 537, K. 595. The tuttis range in length from $1\frac{1}{2}$ to 23 bars, with about half of them being 6–8 bars long.

20 Letter of 20 March 1939 to Aaron Copland, in *Selected Letters of Virgil Thomson*, ed. Tim Page and Vanessa Weeks Page (New York: Summit Books, 1988), p. 127.

21 On the "emphasis on fragments, effects, and localized musical environments" in Mozart's aesthetic, see V. Kofi Agawu, "Mozart's Art of Variation: Remarks on the First Movement of K. 503," in *Mozart's Piano Concertos: Text, Context, Interpretation*, ed. Zaslaw, pp. 303–13.

3 First movements

1 Rosen, *The Classical Style*, p. 233.

2 Olivier Messiaen, *Les 22 concertos pour piano de Mozart* (Paris: Séguier, 1990), p. 78.

3 Ellwood Derr, "Mozart's Transfer of the Vocal 'fermata sospesa' to His Piano-Concerto First Movements," *Mozart-Jahrbuch 1991*, I:155–63. On solo expositions that begin with "new" material see also David Rosen, "'Unexpectedness' and 'Inevitability' in Mozart's Piano Concertos," in *Mozart's Piano Concertos: Text, Context, Interpretation*, ed. Zaslaw, pp. 261–84, especially pp. 270–4. Though we may usefully label and categorize these non-normative solo entries, each remains a special case.

4 Rosen, *The Classical Style*, p. 233–4. Compare the piano opening at bar 77 (Fig. 1: *N*) with the first-movement themes at bars 33 (ritornello "lyric theme," Fig. 1: *4*) and 128 (exposition "second theme," Fig. 1: *D*) and with the last-movement themes at bars 1 ("refrain" theme, Fig. 7: *A¹*) and 63 (solo "reentry" theme, Fig. 7: *E*).

5 Frederick Neumann, *Ornamentation and Improvisation in Mozart* (Princeton, N.J.: Princeton University Press, 1986), p. 16.

6 As Girdlestone points out (*Mozart's Piano Concertos*, p. 315), Mozart also used this plan in the first movement of his Piano Concerto in C Minor, K. 491, as did Beethoven in his Violin Concerto, Op. 61.

7 The tempo marking "Allegro maestoso" is lacking in the autograph but is indicated by Mozart in his thematic catalogue, the *Verzeichnüss* (British Library, Stefan Zweig MS 63), published in facsimile as *Mozart's Thematic Catalogue* (Ithaca, N.Y.: Cornell University Press, 1990).

8 Rosen, *The Classical Style*, p. 236.

9 The solo entrance in K. 503 is similar, though in that concerto the repeated *authentic* cadences by the orchestra seem less like invitations than like cues or prompts, prodding the solo with reminders that the ritornello is indeed over.

10 The concerto was published posthumously in 1800 by Breitkopf & Härtel, Leipzig. The autograph score is in the Dannie and Hettie Heineman Collection of the Pierpont Morgan Library (Heineman MS 266). A facsimile has been published: Mozart, *Piano Concerto No. 21 in C Major, K. 467: The Autograph Score*, The Pierpont Morgan Library Music Manuscript Reprint Series (New York: The Pierpont Morgan Library in association with Dover Publications, 1985). See also the *Neue Mozart-Ausgabe, Kritischer Bericht*, V/15/6, 43–8.

11 See Jan LaRue, "Introduction," in Mozart, *Piano Concerto No. 21 in C Major, K. 467: The Autograph Score*, Fig. 13 on p. xiv.

4 Middle movements

1 See Hans Tischler, *A Structural Analysis of Mozart's Piano Concertos*, pp. 129–30, for a summary of the forms found in Mozart's piano concertos. Throughout the volume, as footnotes to his individual analyses, Tischler indicates the terms used by Girdlestone and Hutchings to describe the forms whenever they differ from his own.

2 *Ibid.*, p. 130.

3 The Romanze in A-flat for solo piano, K. Anh. 205, is spurious.

4 Daniel Heartz, "The Beginnings of the Operatic Romance: Rousseau, Sedaine, and Monsigny," *Eighteenth-Century Studies* 15 (1981–2): 156–7.

5 Thomas Bauman and Julian Budden, "Romance," *The New Grove Dictionary of Opera* (1992), IV:16.

6 Roger Hickman, "Romance," *The New Grove Dictionary of Music and Musicians* (1980), XVI:123–5.

7 Koch, *Introductory Essay on Composition*, p. 212.

8 Heartz, "The Beginnings of the Operatic Romance," p. 157.

9 A sketch of the opening theme from the middle movement of K. 537 is in fact

labeled "Romance," but the movement is untitled in the autograph, where the tempo marking "Larghetto" is not in Mozart's hand.

10 The autograph is in the Gesellschaft der Musikfreunde, Vienna. The Concerto was published posthumously in 1796, in separate editions by Artaria of Vienna and J. André of Offenbach. See the *Neue Mozart-Ausgabe, Kritischer Bericht*, V/15/6, 12–16.

11 Hutchings, *A Companion to Mozart's Piano Concertos*, p. 132.

12 Rosen, *The Classical Style*, p. 235.

13 Eva Badura-Skoda, "Aspects of Performance Practice," in *Eighteenth-Century Keyboard Music*, ed. Marshall, pp. 44–5.

14 Daniel Gottlob Türk, *School of Clavier Playing or Instructions in Playing the Clavier for Teachers & Students*, trans. Raymond H. Haggh (Lincoln and London: University of Nebraska Press, 1982), p. 391.

15 Leonard Maltin, ed., *Leonard Maltin's TV Movies and Video Guide: 1988 Edition* (New York: New American Library, 1987), p. 284.

16 James Webster, "Are Mozart's Concertos 'Dramatic'? Concerto Ritornellos versus Aria Introductions in the 1780s," in *Mozart's Piano Concertos: Text, Context, Interpretation*, ed. Zaslaw, pp. 113 and 127. See the diagram of the movement in his Ex. 3, pp. 128–29.

17 In *Mozart's Piano Concertos: Text, Context, Interpretation*, ed. Zaslaw, pp. 315–33. This article can be enthusiastically recommended, even to those who are normally allergic to Schenkerian analysis.

18 There is, admittedly, an important thematic connection between the orchestral and solo closing themes (*6* and *E*), but that is not the point.

19 See Weising, *Die Sonatenform in den langsamen Konzertsätzen Mozarts*, and Brück, *Die langsamen Sätze in Mozarts Klavierkonzerten*.

20 Mozart used a similar scoring – muted violins and pizzicato lower strings – in the second movement of his Piano Concerto in B-flat, K. 238, of 1776.

21 See Jens Peter Larsen's discussion of the "three-part" exposition in works by Haydn, in the article "Sonata Form Problems," reprinted in Larsen, *Handel, Haydn, and the Viennese Classical Style*, trans. Ulrich Krämer (Ann Arbor: UMI Research Press, 1988), pp. 269–79.

22 Girdlestone, *Mozart's Piano Concertos*, p. 345.

5 Finales

1 Koch, *Introductory Essay on Composition*, p. 213.

2 Joel Galand, "Rondo-Form Problems in Eighteenth- and Nineteenth-Century Instrumental Music, with Reference to the Application of Schenker's Form Theory to Historical Criticism" (Ph.D. diss., Yale Uni-

versity, 1990), p. 141. My discussion of Mozart's concerto rondos and, in particular, the finale of K. 466 is indebted to Galand, especially pp. 151–63 and 174–320. Likewise, the terms "refrain complex" and "re-entry theme" are drawn from this valuable study.

3 Donald Francis Tovey, *The Forms of Music* (1944, as *Musical Articles from the Encyclopaedia Britannica*; rpt. New York: World Publishing Company, 1956), p. 193.

4 Tovey, *Essays in Musical Analysis*, vol. 3, *Concertos*, p. 41.

5 Rosen, *The Classical Style*, pp. 213 and 275.

6 This fragment is reproduced in its entirety in *NMA* V/15/6, 269. Wanda Landowska used the first thirty-one bars of this discarded draft in her cadenza for the definitive finale of K. 466 (New York: Broude Brothers, 1963).

7 The same type of "linkage" between the refrain cadence and the solo re-entry theme may be observed in the finales of K. 459 and K. 503 and, more obliquely, in that of K. 595.

8 See Rosen, *The Classical Style*, pp. 233–5, especially the music examples on p. 234.

9 This argument is advanced with respect to Mozart's so-called "amplified binary" rondo forms (of which the K. 466 finale is an example) by John Daverio in "From 'Concertante Rondo' to 'Lyric Sonata': A Commentary on Brahms's Reception of Mozart," in *Brahms Studies*, ed. David Brodbeck (Lincoln and London: University of Nebraska Press, 1994), I:115–17.

10 On secondary developments, see Rosen, *Sonata Forms*, pp. 289–96.

11 David Grayson, "Whose Authenticity? Ornaments by Hummel and Cramer for Mozart's Piano Concertos," in *Mozart's Piano Concertos: Text, Context, Interpretation*, ed. Zaslaw, p. 386.

12 Wye J. Allanbrook, "Mozart's Tunes and the Comedy of Closure," in *On Mozart*, ed. Morris, pp. 185–6. See also her discussion of the coda theme on p. 185, as well as her comments in "Comic Issues in Mozart's Piano Concertos," in *Mozart's Piano Concertos: Text, Context, Interpretation*, ed. Zaslaw, pp. 99–102.

13 The terms "summarizing coda" and "condensed reprise" are from Daverio, p. 120.

14 Charles Rosen, in *Sonata Forms*, pp. 126–30, uses the concept of a "recapitulation in reverse" to describe the somewhat similar sonata-rondo finales of the Piano Sonata in C major, K. 309/284b, and the Viola Quintet in G minor, K. 516. He distinguishes these from the finale of the Viola Quintet in C major, K. 515, which he considers a "slow-movement form," with the development occupying the position of a secondary development.

15 Rosen, *The Classical Style*, p. 213.

16 Maynard Solomon, *Mozart: A Life* (New York: HarperCollins, 1995), p. 368.

17 The horn parts in bars 60–2 were inexplicably omitted from the first complete edition of Mozart's collected works (1877–1905) and consequently also from its widely distributed reprints.

18 A note to pianists: Robert Levin has suggested that the right-hand octaves in this theme (in bars 143–4 and 149–50 and, later, in bars 394–5 and 400–1) might be Mozart's shorthand notation for *broken* octaves. He advanced the same argument with greater conviction with respect to bars 302 and 304–6. See Levin, "Concertos," in *The Mozart Compendium: A Guide to Mozart's Life and Music*, ed. H. C. Robbins Landon (New York: Schirmer Books, 1990), p. 267.

6 Performance practice issues

1 For a useful overview of performance practice issues relevant to Mozart's music, see Robin Stowell, "Performance Practice," in *The Mozart Compendium*, ed. Robbins Landon, pp. 372–83.

2 Leopold Mozart, *A Treatise on the Fundamental Principles of Violin Playing*, trans. Editha Knocker, 2nd edn. (London: Oxford University Press, 1951); C. P. E. Bach, *Essay on the True Art of Playing Keyboard Instruments*, trans. and ed. William J. Mitchell (New York: W. W. Norton, 1949); and Türk, *School of Clavier Playing*, trans. Haggh.

The specific Türk examples are from *School of Clavier Playing*, pp. 230 and 314–16. Much of the latter example is also reproduced in Robert D. Levin, "Instrumental Ornamentation, Improvisation and Cadenzas," in *Performance Practice: Music after 1600*, ed. Howard Mayer Brown and Stanley Sadie (New York and London: W. W. Norton, 1990), pp. 270–1.

3 Gustav Schilling, *Enzyklopädie der gesamten musikalischen Wissenschaften*, rev. edn. (Stuttgart, 1840), III:606–8. See Philipp Karl Hoffmann, *Cadenzas to Mozart's Piano Concertos and Elaborations of Their Slow Movements*, ed. A. Hyatt King (London: Peters, 1959), pp. 4–5.

4 Neumann, *Ornamentation and Improvisation in Mozart*, p. 247.

5 Maynard Solomon, "The Rochlitz Anecdotes: Issues of Authenticity in Early Mozart Biography," in *Mozart Studies*, ed. Cliff Eisen (Oxford: Oxford University Press, 1991), p. 25.

6 See Henry G. Mishkin, "Incomplete Notation in Mozart's Piano Concertos," *Musical Quarterly* 61 (1975): 345–59.

7 Linda Faye Ferguson offers alternative explanations of the Rochlitz anecdote in " 'Col Basso' and 'Generalbass' in Mozart's Keyboard Concertos: Nota-

tion, Performance Theory, and Practice" (Ph.D. diss., Princeton University, 1983), pp. 85–91.

8 Much, but not all, of this final draft is offered as a "second version" in Hermann Beck's edition for the *Neue Mozart Ausgabe*; the "standard" edition is therefore actually Mozart's penultimate version. Given the relative simplicity and inferiority of parts of the final sketch version, we should not rule out the possibility that it was prepared as an easier alternative for a less skilled pianist, perhaps a student. See Robert Levin's critique of the Beck edition in "The Devil's in the Details: Neglected Aspects of Mozart's Piano Concertos," in *Mozart's Piano Concertos: Text, Context, Interpretation*, ed. Zaslaw, pp. 29–50.

9 Anderson, ed., *The Letters of Mozart and His Family*, no. 515, p. 880.

10 This important document has been frequently reproduced, including: the Köchel catalogue (6th edn.); Eva Badura-Skoda and Paul Badura-Skoda, *Interpreting Mozart on the Keyboard*, trans. Leo Black (New York: St. Martin's Press, 1962), p. 178; *Neue Mozart Ausgabe*, V/15/5, p. 208; Levin, "Improvisation and Embellishment in Mozart Piano Concertos," p. 7; Neumann, *Ornamentation and Improvisation in Mozart*, p. 241; Levin, "Instrumental Ornamentation, Improvisation and Cadenzas," p. 277; and Levin, "Mozart's Keyboard Concertos," p. 367.

11 Notes to his 1955 recording of Mozart's Piano Concertos, K. 451 and 488, with Alexander Schneider conducting the Columbia Symphony Orchestra (Columbia Records, ML 5297).

12 Neumann, *Ornamentation and Improvisation in Mozart*, p. 251. The embellished Adagio is reproduced, in transcription and facsimile, in the *Neue Mozart Ausgabe, Kritischer Bericht*, V/15/7, pp. 10–14 and 106–9.

13 The Cramer and Hummel editions are the subject of David Grayson, "Whose Authenticity? Ornaments by Hummel and Cramer for Mozart's Piano Concertos," in *Mozart's Piano Concertos: Text, Context, Interpretation*, ed. Zaslaw, pp. 373–91.

14 See, for example, Neumann, *Ornamentation and Improvisation in Mozart*, pp. 247 and 251–3, and Joseph Kerman, "Mozart à la Mode," p. 52.

15 Landowska's classic 1937 studio recording of the "Coronation" Concerto, K. 537, is currently available on a Biddulph compact disc (LHW 013), while her 1945–6 concert performances of the Piano Concertos in C, K. 415, and in E-flat, K. 482, are on Music & Arts CD-821. Landowska's embellishments for K. 482 and K. 537 were published in 1963 by Broude Brothers, New York. Of Gulda's recordings, I am thinking not of his relatively restrained more recent collaborations with Abbado and Harnoncourt, but of his more "daring" 1960s recording of the Piano Concertos in C, K. 467, and B-flat, K. 595, with

Hans Swarowsky and the Vienna State Opera Orchestra, reissued on Preiser CD 90021. Eva Badura-Skoda's transcription of a passage from this Gulda recording (K. 467, movement 2, bars 58–71) is an object lesson in the shortcomings of notated representations of improvisations, as it fails to reflect the pianist's rhythmic liberties, particularly the degree to which his two hands are unsynchronized; see her "On Improvised Embellishments and Cadenzas in Mozart's Piano Concertos," in *Mozart's Piano Concertos: Text, Context, Interpretation*, ed. Zaslaw, p. 368.

16 See Badura-Skoda, *Interpreting Mozart*, pp. 180–2; Levin, "Improvisation and Embellishment in Mozart Piano Concertos," pp. 7–8; Neumann, *Ornamentation and Improvisation in Mozart*, pp. 233–8; and Levin, "Improvised Embellishments in Mozart's Keyboard Music," *Early Music* 20 (1992): 224–7.

17 Levin, "Instrumental Ornamentation, Improvisation and Cadenzas," p. 272. See Levin, "Improvised Embellishments in Mozart's Keyboard Music," pp. 223–4, where Example 1 aligns the five appearances of the main theme of K. 511.

18 See, for example, Neumann, *Ornamentation and Improvisation in Mozart*, p. 252 ("Ployer's stock device of a dashing chromatic scale . . . , wiping out the silver bells as with a sweep of a mop, is an abomination"); or Kerman, "Mozart à la Mode," p. 52 ("The atrocious chromatic runs in this source should give pause to even the most hardened historical reconstructor").

19 Levin, "Improvisation and Embellishment in Mozart Piano Concertos," pp. 9–11, and "Instrumental Ornamentation, Improvisation and Cadenzas," pp. 276–9.

20 Gustav Leonhardt, "On the Use of Original Instruments," trans. Robert Jordan, notes to LP recording of J. S. Bach, Six Brandenburg Concertos, BWV 1046–1051, Pro-Arte 2PAX-2001 (1980).

21 Christoph Wolff, "Cadenzas and Styles of Improvisation in Mozart's Piano Concertos," in *Perspectives on Mozart Performance*, ed. Todd and Williams, pp. 230–1.

22 Philip Whitmore, *Unpremeditated Art: The Cadenza in the Classical Keyboard Concerto* (Oxford: Oxford University Press, 1991), p. 142.

23 Christoph Wolff, "Zur Chronologie der Klavierkonzert-Kadenzen Mozarts," *Mozart-Jahrbuch 1978/79*, pp. 236–7 and 240–2.

24 Anderson, ed., *The Letters of Mozart and His Family*, no. 516, p. 881.

25 Anderson, ed., *The Letters of Mozart and His Family*, no. 479, p. 837.

26 A similar argument has been advanced by Peter Kivy in *Authenticities* (Ithaca and London: Cornell University Press, 1995), pp. 273–6.

27 Badura-Skoda, *Interpreting Mozart*, Chapter 11. Paul Badura-Skoda put this

"formula" into practice in a volume of cadenzas and lead-ins, plus some slow-movement embellishments, published in 1967 by Bärenreiter. He consistently deferred to the composer in declining to offer such additions where Mozart's own survive.

28 Tovey, "Prefaces to Cadenzas for Classical Concertos," in *Essays and Lectures on Music* (reprinted as *The Main Stream of Music and Other Essays*), ed. Hubert Foss (London: Oxford University Press, 1949), p. 315.

29 The most thorough treatment of the subject is Ferguson, "'Col Basso' and 'Generalbass' in Mozart's Keyboard Concertos." Some of Ferguson's conclusions also appear in the articles "Mozart's Keyboard Concertos: Tutti Notations and Performance Models," *Mozart-Jahrbuch 1984/85*, pp. 32–9, and "The Classical Keyboard Concerto: Some Thoughts on Authentic Performance," *Early Music* 12 (1984): 437–45.

30 Levin, "Improvisation and Embellishment in Mozart Piano Concertos," pp. 3–4.

31 A listing of the "authentic" manuscript and printed sources of Mozart's piano concertos, with indications of which contain figured bass, constitutes Appendix A of Ferguson, "'Col Basso' and 'Generalbass' in Mozart's Keyboard Concertos," pp. 323–7.

32 Badura-Skoda, *Interpreting Mozart*, pp. 199–201; Derr, "*Basso Continuo* in Mozart's Piano Concertos: Dimensions of Compositional Completion and Performance Practice," in *Mozart's Piano Concertos: Text, Context, Interpretation*, ed. Zaslaw, pp. 393–410.

33 Rosen, *The Classical Style*, p. 196.

34 Rosen, *The Classical Style*, p. 192. Had he wished to offer supporting evidence he might have cited the "thinly scored" texture of the Piano Concerto in A, K. 414/385p, third movement, bars 71–3, where the scoring and piano writing preclude the addition of basso continuo, demonstrating that the "thin" texture in this case was precisely what Mozart must have wanted. Robert Levin challenged Rosen's assertion in "Improvisation and Embellishment in Mozart's Piano Concertos," p. 4.

35 Ferguson, "'Col Basso' and 'Generalbass' in Mozart's Keyboard Concertos," pp. 13–15. Ferguson offers evidence contradicting Rosen's hypothesis in "Mozart's Keyboard Concertos: Tutti Notations and Performance Models," pp. 34–6.

36 Badura-Skoda, *Interpreting Mozart*, p. 198. Neumann, *Ornamentation and Improvisation in Mozart*, pp. 254–5. Paul Badura-Skoda's edition of K. 246 (Eulenburg) includes Mozart's continuo realization, as does Christoph Wolff's *NMA* edition.

37 See Badura-Skoda. *Interpreting Mozart*, pp. 207–8, for the authors' "gener-

ally valid rules for continuo playing in Mozart," based on the composer's continuo realization for K. 246.

38 Levin, "Improvisation and Embellishment in Mozart Piano Concertos," pp. 5–6.

39 Neumann, *Ornamentation and Improvisation in Mozart*, p. 255.

40 Neal Zaslaw, notes to *Piano Concertos, K. 415/387b and K. 450*, recording by Malcolm Bilson, with John Eliot Gardiner conducting the English Baroque Soloists (Archiv CD 413 464–2; Hamburg, 1984).

41 Rosen, *The Classical Style*, p.193.

42 Levin, "Improvisation and Embellishment in Mozart Piano Concertos," p. 5.

43 Peter Shaffer, *Amadeus*, film edition (New York: New American Library, 1984), p. 46. Otto Erich Deutsch, ed., *Mozart: A Documentary Biography*, trans. Eric Blom, Peter Branscombe, and Jeremy Noble, 2nd edn. (Stanford: Stanford University Press, 1966), pp. 499.

44 Most of this section is indebted to Richard Maunder and David Rowland, "Mozart's Pedal Piano," *Early Music* 23 (1995): 287–96.

45 Anderson, ed., *The Letters of Mozart and His Family*, no. 525, p. 889.

46 Deutsch, ed., *Mozart: A Documentary Biography*, pp. 325–6.

47 *Ibid.*, p. 561.

48 Cliff Eisen, ed., *New Mozart Documents* (Stanford: Stanford University Press, 1991), p. 39.

49 Deutsch, ed., *Mozart: A Documentary Biography*, p. 586.

50 Levin, "Mozart's Keyboard Concertos," in *Eighteenth-Century Keyboard Music*, p. 391.

51 Maunder and Rowland, "Mozart's Pedal Piano," pp. 291–2.

52 Neal Zaslaw, "Contexts for Mozart's Piano Concertos," in *Mozart's Piano Concertos: Text, Context, Interpretation*, ed. Zaslaw, pp. 13–15.

53 Anderson, ed., *The Letters of Mozart and His Family*, no. 513, p. 877.

54 Deutsch, ed., *Mozart: A Documentary Biography*, p. 212.

55 Daniel Heartz, *Haydn, Mozart and the Viennese School: 1740–1780* (New York: Norton, 1995), p. 62.

56 Morrow, *Concert Life in Haydn's Vienna*, p. 53.

57 Anderson, ed., *The Letters of Mozart and His Family*, nos. 523 and 525, pp. 885 and 888.

58 Otto Biba, "Concert Life in Beethoven's Vienna," in *Beethoven, Performers, and Critics: The International Beethoven Congress, Detroit, 1977*, ed. Robert Winter and Bruce Carr (Detroit: Wayne State University Press, 1980), p. 93.

59 Zaslaw, "Contexts for Mozart's Piano Concertos," p. 14.

60 Andreas Streicher, *Kurze Bemerkungen über das Spielen, Stimmen und Erhal-*

ten der Forte-Piano, welche von Nannette Streicher geborne Stein in Wien verfertiget werden, ausschliessend nur für Besitzer dieser Instrumente aufgesetzt (Vienna, 1801), p. 26; quoted in Zaslaw, "Contexts for Mozart's Piano Concertos," p. 14. Translated into English in *Brief Remarks on the Playing, Tuning and Care of Fortepianos Made in Vienna by Nannette Streicher née Stein, Prepared Exclusively for the Owners of These Instruments*, trans. Preethi de Silva (Ann Arbor: Early Music Facsimiles, 1983).

61 Morrow, *Concert Life in Haydn's Vienna*, p. 187.

62 Deutsch, ed., *Mozart: A Documentary Biography*, p. 559.

63 Morrow, *Concert Life in Haydn's Vienna*, p. 73. For information regarding the Burgtheater, see also Heartz, *Haydn, Mozart and the Viennese School*, pp. 33–41; Heartz, "Nicolas Jadot and the Building of the Burgtheater," *Musical Quarterly* 68 (1982): 1–31; and Otto G. Schindler, "Das Publikum des Burgtheaters in der Josephinischen Ära," in *Das Burgtheater und sein Publikum*, ed. Margret Dietrich (Vienna: Verlag der Österreichischen Akademie der Wissenschaften, 1976), pp. 11–95.

64 Heartz, *Haydn, Mozart and the Viennese School*, p. 41.

65 Biba, "Concert Life in Beethoven's Vienna," p. 83; Morrow, *Concert Life in Haydn's Vienna*, p. 75.

66 *Allgemeiner Theater Almanach vom Jahre 1782*, cited in Morrow, p. 175.

67 Salzburg, Abbey of St Peter, MS Moz 275.1. See the description of these parts in Horst Heussner's *Kritischer Bericht* for the *Neue Mozart Ausgabe* V/15/6, pp. 13–15. They are also discussed in Cliff Eisen, "The Mozarts' Salzburg Copyists: Aspects of Attribution, Chronology, Text, Style, and Performance Practice," in *Mozart Studies*, ed. Eisen, pp. 295–8; and Eisen, "The Scoring of the Orchestral Bass Part in Mozart's Salzburg Keyboard Concertos," in *Mozart's Piano Concertos: Text, Context, Interpretation*, ed. Zaslaw, p. 416.

68 See Christoph Wolff, "Über kompositionsgeschichtlichen Ort und Aufführungspraxis der Klavierkonzerts Mozarts," *Mozart-Jahrbuch 1986*, pp. 91–2.

69 Translated in Dexter Edge, "Manuscript Parts as Evidence of Orchestral Size in the Eighteenth-Century Viennese Concerto," in *Mozart's Piano Concertos: Text, Context, Interpretation*, ed. Zaslaw, p. 440.

70 Edge, Table 1 on p. 436, and p. 446.

71 Neal Zaslaw, notes to *Piano Concertos, K. 415/387b and K. 450.*

72 Richard Maunder, "Performing Mozart and Beethoven Concertos," *Early Music* 17 (1989): 139–40.

73 Heartz, "Nicolas Jadot and the Building of the Burgtheater," pp. 23–6.

74 Morrow, *Concert Life in Haydn's Vienna*, pp. 183–4.

Select Bibliography

Anderson, Emily, trans. and ed. *The Letters of Mozart and His Family*, 3rd edn. (New York and London: W. W. Norton, 1985)

Badura-Skoda, Eva, and Paul Badura-Skoda. *Interpreting Mozart on the Keyboard*, trans. Leo Black (New York: St. Martin's Press, 1962)

Bonds, Mark Evan. *Wordless Rhetoric: Musical Form and the Metaphor of the Oration* (Cambridge, Mass. and London: Harvard University Press, 1991)

Brown, Howard Mayer, and Stanley Sadie, eds. *Performance Practice: Music after 1600* (New York and London: W. W. Norton, 1990)

Brück, Marion. *Die langsamen Sätze in Mozarts Klavierkonzerten. Untersuchungen zur Form und zum musikalischen Satz*, Studien zur Musik, no. 12 (Munich: Wilhelm Fink, 1994)

Daverio, John. "From 'Concertante Rondo' to 'Lyric Sonata': A Commentary on Brahms's Reception of Mozart," in *Brahms Studies*, vol. 1, ed. David Brodbeck (Lincoln and London: University of Nebraska Press, 1994)

Davis, Shelley. "H. C. Koch, the Classic Concerto, and the Sonata-Form Retransition," *Journal of Musicology* 2 (1983): 45–61

Derr, Ellwood. "Mozart's Transfer of the Vocal 'fermata sospesa' to His Piano-Concerto First Movements," *Mozart-Jahrbuch 1991*, I:155–63

Eisen, Cliff, ed. *Mozart Studies* (Oxford: Oxford University Press, 1991)

Ferguson, Linda Faye. "'Col Basso' and 'Generalbass' in Mozart's Keyboard Concertos: Notation, Performance Theory, and Practice" (Ph.D. diss., Princeton University, 1983)

"The Classical Keyboard Concerto: Some Thoughts on Authentic Performance," *Early Music* 12 (1984): 437–45

"Mozart's Keyboard Concertos: Tutti Notations and Performance Models," *Mozart-Jahrbuch 1984/85*, pp. 32–39

Forman, Denis. *Mozart's Concerto Form: The First Movements of the Piano Concertos* (New York: Praeger, 1971)

Galand, Joel. "Rondo-Form Problems in Eighteenth- and Nineteenth-

Century Instrumental Music, with Reference to the Application of Schenker's Form Theory to Historical Criticism" (Ph.D. diss., Yale University, 1990)

Girdlestone, Cuthbert M. *Mozart's Piano Concertos*, 2nd edn. (London: Cassel, 1958)

Heartz, Daniel. *Haydn, Mozart and the Viennese School: 1740–1780* (New York: Norton, 1995)

Hutchings, Arthur. *A Companion to Mozart's Piano Concertos*, 2nd edn. (London: Oxford University Press, 1950)

Kerman, Joseph. "Mozart's Piano Concertos and Their Audience," in *On Mozart*, ed. James M. Morris (Cambridge: Woodrow Wilson Center Press and Cambridge University Press, 1994), pp. 151–68; rpt. in Kerman, *Write All These Down: Essays on Music* (Berkeley: University of California Press, 1994), pp. 322–34

"Mozart à la Mode," *New York Review of Books*, 18 May 1989, pp. 50–52

Koch, Heinrich Joseph. *Introductory Essay on Composition [1782–93]: The Mechanical Rules of Melody, Sections 3 and 4*, trans. Nancy Kovaleff Baker (New Haven and London: Yale University Press, 1983)

Kramer, Richard. "Cadenza Contra Text: Mozart in Beethoven's Hands," *19th-Century Music* 15 (1991): 116–31

Küster, Konrad. *Formale Aspekte des ersten Allegros in Mozarts Konzerten* (Kassel: Bärenreiter, 1991)

Landon, H. C. Robbins, ed. *The Mozart Compendium: A Guide to Mozart's Life and Music* (New York: Schirmer Books, 1990)

Landon, H. C. Robbins, and Donald Mitchell, eds. *The Mozart Companion* (London: Rockliff, 1956)

Leeson, Daniel N., and Robert D. Levin. "On the Authenticity of K. Anh. C14.01 (297b), a Symphonia Concertante for Four Winds and Orchestra," *Mozart-Jahrbuch 1976/77*, pp. 70–96

Levin, Robert D. "Improvisation and Embellishment in Mozart Piano Concertos," *Musical Newsletter* 5, no. 2 (1975): 3–14

"Improvisation and Musical Structure in the Mozart Concerti," in *L'interprétation de la musique classique de Haydn à Schubert: Colloque international, Evry, 13–15 octobre 1977* (Paris: Fondation pour l'art & la recherche and Editions Minkoff, 1980), pp. 45–55

"Improvised Embellishments in Mozart's Keyboard Music," *Early Music* 20 (1992): 221–33

"Instrumental Ornamentation, Improvisation and Cadenzas," in *Performances Practice: Music after 1600*, ed. Howard Mayer Brown and Stanley Sadie (New York and London: W. W. Norton, 1990), pp. 267–91

"Mozart's Keyboard Concertos," in *Eighteenth-Century Keyboard Music*, ed. Robert L. Marshall (New York: Schirmer Books, 1994)

Who Wrote the Mozart Four-Wind Concertante? (Stuyvesant, N.Y.: Pendragon Press, 1988)

Marshall, Robert L., ed. *Eighteenth-Century Keyboard Music* (New York: Schirmer Books, 1994)

Maunder, Richard. "Performance Problems in Mozart's Keyboard Concertos," *Mozart-Jahrbuch 1991*, I:319–26

Maunder, Richard, and David Rowland. "Mozart's Pedal Piano," *Early Music* 23 (1995): 287–96

McClary, Susan. "A Musical Dialectic from the Enlightenment: Mozart's *Piano Concerto in G Major, K. 453*, Movement 2," *Cultural Critique* 4 (1986): 129–69

Messiaen, Olivier. *Les 22 concertos pour piano de Mozart* (Paris: Séguier, 1990)

Mishkin, Henry G. "Incomplete Notation in Mozart's Piano Concertos," *Musical Quarterly* 61 (1975): 345–59

Morris, James M., ed. *On Mozart* (Cambridge: Woodrow Wilson Center Press and Cambridge University Press, 1994)

Morrow, Mary Sue. *Concert Life in Haydn's Vienna: Aspects of a Developing Musical and Social Institution* (Stuyvesant, N.Y.: Pendragon Press, 1989)

Mozart, Wolfgang Amadeus. *Piano Concerto No. 21 in C Major, K. 467: The Autograph Score*, The Pierpont Morgan Library Music Manuscript Reprint Series, ed. J. Rigbie Turner and Stanley Appelbaum (New York: The Pierpont Morgan Library in association with Dover Publications, 1985)

Neumann, Frederick. *Ornamentation and Improvisation in Mozart* (Princeton, N.J.: Princeton University Press, 1986)

Radcliffe, Philip. *Mozart Piano Concertos* (London: BBC Publications, 1978)

Rosen, Charles. *The Classical Style*, expanded edn. (New York: Norton, 1997)

Sonata Forms, rev. edn. (New York: Norton, 1988)

Simon, Edwin J. "The Double Exposition in the Classic Concerto," *Journal of the American Musicological Society* 10 (1957): 111–18

Solomon, Maynard. *Mozart: A Life* (New York: HarperCollins, 1995)

Stevens, Jane R. "An 18th-Century Description of Concerto First-Movement Form," *Journal of the American Musicological Society* 24 (1971): 85–95

"Theme, Harmony, and Texture in Classic–Romantic Descriptions of Concerto First-Movement Form," *Journal of the American Musicological Society* 27 (1974): 25–60

Taruskin, Richard. *Text and Act: Essays on Music and Performance* (Oxford: Oxford University Press, 1995)

Tischler, Hans. *A Structural Analysis of Mozart's Piano Concertos* (Brooklyn, New York: Institute of Medieval Music, 1966)

Todd, R. Larry, and Peter Williams, eds. *Perspectives on Mozart Performance* (Cambridge: Cambridge University Press, 1991)

Tovey, Donald Francis. *Essays and Lectures on Music* (reprinted as *The Main Stream of Music and Other Essays*), ed. Hubert Foss (London: Oxford University Press, 1949)

    Essays in Musical Analysis, 7 vols. (London: Oxford University Press, 1935–44)

    The Forms of Music (1944, as *Musical Articles from the Encyclopaedia Britannica*; rpt. New York: World Publishing Company, 1956)

Weising, Klaus. *Die Sonatenform in den langsamen Konzertsätzen Mozarts* (Hamburg: Karl Dieter Wagner, 1970)

Whitmore, Philip. *Unpremeditated Art: The Cadenza in the Classical Keyboard Concerto* (Oxford: Oxford University Press, 1991)

Wolff, Christoph. "Über kompositionsgeschichtlichen Ort und Aufführungspraxis der Klavierkonzerts Mozarts," *Mozart-Jahrbuch 1986*, pp. 91–92

    "Zur Chronologie der Klavierkonzert-Kadenzen Mozarts," *Mozart-Jahrbuch 1978/79*, pp. 235–46

Zaslaw, Neal, ed. *Mozart's Piano Concertos: Text, Context, Interpretation* (Ann Arbor: University of Michigan Press, 1996)

Index

Abbado, Claudio, 129n
Alkan, Charles, 1
Allanbrook, Wye Jamison, 84
Amadeus (Peter Shaffer), 108
amplified binary form, 85
Anda, Geza, 63
ars combinatoria, 9–10
Atwood, Thomas, 109

Bach, Carl Philipp Emanuel, 7, 95–6,
    119n, 122n, 123n
Bach, Johann Christian, 7, 16, 20, 21,
    119n, 120–1n, 122n
Bach, Johann Sebastian, 7, 12–13, 109,
    119n, 122n
  Mass in B minor, BWV 232, 32
  Concerto for Violin and Orchestra in
    E, BWV 1042, 74
Badura-Skoda, Eva, 96, 103, 104, 106,
    130n
Badura-Skoda, Paul, 96, 103, 104, 106,
    130–1n, 131–2n
basso continuo, *see* performance practice
    issues: basso continuo
Beethoven, Ludwig van, 12, 102, 122n
  cadenzas for K. 466, 1, 32, 40, 43, 83
  concertos for piano and orchestra
    No. 1 in C, Op. 15, 18
    No. 5 in E♭, Op. 73 ("Emperor"), 18
  Concerto for Violin and Orchestra,
    Op. 61, 125n
  Symphony No. 5 in C minor, Op. 67, 1
Bernstein, Leonard, 94
Bilson, Malcolm, 8

Boccherini, Luigi, 20
Bonds, Mark Evan, 14–15, 19, 21
Boulanger, Nadia, xii
Brahms, Johannes, 1, 12, 25, 85
Bréval, Jean-Baptiste, 123n
Bruckner, Anton, 25
Burgtheater, 4, 113–14, 116–17
Busoni, Ferruccio, 1, 102–3

cadenzas and lead-ins (*Eingänge*), *see*
    performance practice issues:
    cadenzas and lead-ins (*Eingänge*)
Cambini, Giuseppe Maria, 123n
Casella, Alfredo, 1
Challis, John, 8
Chopin, Fryderyk Franciszek, 12
Chusid, Martin, 2
concerto/concerto form
  amplified binary form, 85
  Baroque, 7, 9, 12–14, 16, 105
  double exposition, 9, 13–14, 15
  expanded binary form, 85
  finale forms, 14, 73–5
  first movement form, 5, 8–9, 12–30,
    57, 64–5, 73
  middle movement forms, 5, 14, 57–9,
    63–5
  opera and, 7
  re-entry theme, 77, 88, 127n
  refrain complex, 76–7, 81, 88, 90, 92,
    127n
  ritornello form and, 8
  social metaphors, 5–7, 84, 92, 94
  sonata form and, 8–9, 13–14

138

Index

Index

Levin, Robert D., 8, 20, 23, 100–1, 103, 106, 110, 128n, 131n; *see also* Leeson–Levin thematic/structural model
Lubin, Steven, 8

Marchand, Heinrich, 113, 114
Masur, Kurt, 94
Maunder, Richard, 116
McClary, Susan, 5
Mehlgrube, 3–4, 108–9, 112–13, 114
Mendelssohn, Felix, xii, 1, 12, 118n
Messiaen, Olivier, 32
Michelangeli, Arturo Benedetti, 94
Morrow, Mary Sue, 116
Mozart, Constanze, 6
Mozart, Leopold, 2, 4, 36, 62, 95, 102, 108–9, 111–15
Mozart, Maria Anna ("Nannerl"), 62, 98, 101–2, 108
Mozart, Wolfgang Amadeus
  Concerto for Piano and Orchestra in D minor, K. 466
    autograph, 60, 76, 110, 126n
    cadenzas, 1, 32, 40, 43, 83, 101, 127n
    composition of, 1–2, 3, 60, 76, 110
    embellishment of Romance, 62–3
    finale (first version), 76, 77
    first edition, 126n
    manuscript parts, 114–16, 133n
    pedal piano and, 81, 109–11
    performed by Mozart, 4, 109–10, 112–13
    social metaphors, 84
    tempo of Romance, 62
  Concerto for Piano and Orchestra in C major, K. 467
    autograph, 4, 48, 125n
    cadenzas, 1, 5, 56, 101
    composition of, 1–2, 3, 4, 48
    counterpoint in, 3
    Elvira Madigan and, 1, 63, 72
    embellishment of Andante, 96
    first edition, 125
    pedal piano and, 108–9, 111

  performed by Mozart, 4, 108–9, 113
  other works
    Betulia liberata, La, K. 118/74c, 3
    "Ch'io mi scordi di te . . . Non temer amato bene," K. 505, 109–10
    Clarinet Quintet in B♭, K. Anh. 91/516c, 123
    Concerto for Bassoon and Orchestra in B♭, K. 191/186e, 27, 74
    Concerto for Clarinet and Orchestra in A, K. 622, 59
    concertos for flute and orchestra: K. 313/285c in G, 26; K. 314/285d in D, 30
    concertos for horn and orchestra: K. 447 in E♭, 57–8, 59; K. 495 in E♭, 57, 59, 61
    Concerto for Oboe and Orchestra in F, K. 293/416f, 123n
    concertos for piano and orchestra:
      K. 107 No. 1 in D, 122n
      K. 175 in D, 27, 73, 102, 124n
      K. 238 in B♭, 30, 124n, 126n
      K. 242 in F, 102, 104, 124n
      K. 246 in C, 104, 106–7, 124n, 131n, 132n
      K. 271 in E♭, 16, 20, 22, 24, 28, 30, 36, 75, 101–2, 122n
      K. 365/316a in E♭, 74, 102, 124n
      K. 382 (Rondo) in D, 73, 102
      K. 413/387a in F, 22, 23, 27–8, 36, 74, 104, 112, 123n
      K. 414/385p in A, 64–5, 74, 104, 112, 124n, 131n
      K. 415/387b in C, 22, 26, 27, 33, 36, 43, 75, 100, 104, 106, 107, 112, 129n
      K. 449 in E♭, 17, 23, 33, 43, 64, 73, 74, 99, 111–12, 124n
      K. 450 in B♭, 7, 25, 28, 30, 36, 111–12, 124n
      K. 451 in D, 24, 27, 30, 32, 73, 74, 98, 100, 111–12
      K. 453 in G, 8, 18, 22, 24, 27, 28, 30, 32, 64, 73, 99, 112, 124n

Index